# Praise for
# A SUMMER IN GASCONY

"Nostalgia for a traditional France, soused in
Armagnac, sunshine and young love, brought
vividly to life."
*John Mole, author of* It's All Greek to Me!

"Entrancing... the reader soaks up Gascony like a
thirsty vine."
*Kevin Gale, France Bookshop*

"Martin's vivid descriptions of his time spent in
*la France profonde* allow readers to experience, eat and
drink their way through a summer in Gascony from
the comfort of an armchair."
*Nick & Karen Kitchener,*
*EARL Domaine de Lauroux Winery*

"A charming and nostalgic account, written in an
accessible and down-to-earth style, this book offers
an insider's perspective of Gascony. I felt entirely
satisfied with this read and keen to sample
Gascony's rural pleasures for myself."
*Becci Sargent, French Magazine Book Club*

# A SUMMER IN GASCONY

## Discovering the *Other*
## South of France

### MARTIN CALDER

**nb**

NICHOLAS BREALEY
PUBLISHING

LONDON · BOSTON

This paperback edition first published by
Nicholas Brealey Publishing in 2009
First published 2008

3–5 Spafield Street
Clerkenwell, London
EC1R 4QB, UK
Tel: +44 (0)20 7239 0360
Fax: +44 (0)20 7239 0370

20 Park Plaza, Suite 1115A
Boston
MA 02116, USA
Tel: (888) BREALEY
Fax: (617) 523 3708

www.nicholasbrealey.com
www.asummeringascony.com

Illustrations by the author.

ISBN: 978-1-85788-531-6

**British Library Cataloguing in Publication Data**
A catalogue record for this book is available from the
British Library.

**FSC**
**Mixed Sources**
Product group from well-managed
forests and other controlled sources
Cert no. SGS - COC - 2061
www.fsc.org
© 1996 Forest Stewardship Council

Printed in the UK by Clays Ltd on
Forest Stewardship Council certified paper.

# CONTENTS

# A SUMMER IN GASCONY

*The real Gascon, with the flashing eyes of the Pyrenees, swarthy of skin, short of stature, gaunt-featured like the earth which clings to the rocks in his country, an original character, full of contradictions, brave as his sword, loud as his drum, embarrassed by praise, humble in the face of criticism, fond of rewarding adventures, ready to give to a profitable cause, careful with his money, liberal with his promises, talkative yet capable of being quiet, irritable yet capable of self-control, ambitious yet patient, as thoughtful as he is hot-headed, as agreeable as he is proud, always master of his heart and his head, even in moments of high emotion, such is the real and authentic Gascon.*

Translated from the French of Charles Normand, 1892

# PROLOGUE

I FIRST DISCOVERED GASCONY DURING A MEMORABLE SUMMER I spent living and working with a farming family in their *ferme-auberge* in a remote hilltop village in southwest France. I was 22 at the time and was on the long university vacation. The summer was a time of challenges and pleasures, as I adapted to an environment completely unfamiliar to me. I came to admire and respect the values and traditions of the Gascon people, and their determination to preserve their way of life in the face of the pressures of the modern world.

The preceding summer I had picked grapes in the Languedoc, on the vineyards of the renowned Blanquette de Limoux, the oldest sparkling wine in France. The *vendange* was interesting, but brutally hard work. I stayed a couple of weeks and the only people I met, apart from minimal contact with the grower, were other British students and a pair of disaffected Scots who worked on the *vendange* every year. I wanted to go back to work in the area, but this time to get to know local people.

The South of France held rich associations. I'd read the books and seen the films *Jean de Florette* and *Manon des Sources*, about peasant life in Provence. I'd been inspired by the film *Betty Blue*, with the quirky life it portrayed at Gruissan-Plage on the Mediterranean coast and in the small town of Marvejols, in the Lozère. I'd been told that Gascony, in the far southwest, was the most rural part of

1

France, where every aspect of life was in some way related to farming and country pursuits.

I'd already had some dealings with an overseas employment agency in Oxford, so I obtained a list of summer work available that year. One advert jumped off the page, a job in the village of Péguilhan in deepest Gascony. The ad gave a few details: a traditional country inn with a separate farm, run by the Cazagnac family, offering good regional food and hospitality. Their business was new and expanding and they needed summer workers to help them during the high season, both at the Auberge itself and on their farm. Just before Easter, I wrote an enthusiastic letter with a passport photograph of myself stapled to the corner, keeping my fingers crossed that something would come of it. A couple of weeks later a letter arrived from the Cazagnacs, saying they would be happy for me to come to work for them. I had a good feeling about it: the Auberge and the farm appealed to my ideas of escapism and adventure, combined with family life. I wrote back straight away, saying I would arrive towards the end of May.

I'd studied civil engineering at university and was following that up with a degree in French. I'm quite practical and my French was good, but nothing qualified me for the work I did that summer. The people and customs of Gascony gave me an abrupt culture shock when I first arrived. And in addition to the hard work and the new people, I had to adapt to living in such an isolated place, far away from home.

That was a few years ago. The Channel Tunnel was being constructed at the time but was not yet open. There were no cheap flights to the southwest of France, nor did the fast train, the TGV, yet serve the area. The only reasonable option was the Channel ferry followed by long train journeys. The euro was only an idea then and price conversions were easy – ten francs to the pound – but in this rural landscape it hardly mattered, there was nowhere to spend what money I earned.

Gascony has a distinct identity and a particular history, which set it apart from the rest of France. It was home to an ancient Iberian tribe called the Vascones, who gave it their name. For centuries it was an independent state ruled by the Dukes of Gascony. It has old affinities and friendships with England. Gascony supplied England with huge quantities of wine, making people in both nations prosperous and happy. In the Middle Ages Gascons fought alongside the English against a common foe – the French! During the Napoleonic Wars, the Gascon peasantry sided with the British army against the French. The Gascons still regard northern France as another country and are particularly suspicious of Parisians.

Stretching from Toulouse in the east to the Atlantic coast in the west, from the river Garonne in the north to the Pyrenees in the south, Gascony is a golden land of rolling hills and wide horizons, swathed with vineyards, sunflowers, maize and pastures. Wild boar and roe deer roam the oak forests. The people are honest, welcoming, earthy, stubborn and independent. In the towns in summer, locals and visitors can join in with the street music of the *joyeuses bandas*, lively brass and percussion orchestras of musicians dressed in colourful costumes. The Gascons have their own particular customs, and the French outside of Gascony, when confronted with their funny ways, shrug their shoulders – *it's the southwest, what can you expect?*

FRANÇA

BORDÈU

GASCONHA

ARCAISHON

GARONA

CONDON

AUSH

TOLOSA

BAIONA

BASCOAT

PAU

SENT GAUDENÇ

PIRENÈUS

4

# A WARM WELCOME

THE BRAKES OF THE OVERNIGHT SLEEPER TRAIN FROM PARIS squealed steadily as it drew into Toulouse Matabiau station just after seven o'clock in the morning. I hadn't slept much during the night: the tip-down couchette had been cramped and not very comfortable, and besides, my mind was too full of expectations about the summer ahead. The train came to a halt as the force of the brakes overcame its awesome momentum. The station was busy, with people criss-crossing between the ticket hall and the platforms. I jumped out of the way of a motorised luggage trolley as it nudged impatiently through the crowd.

I bought a ticket and boarded a local stopping train to take me on the next leg of my journey to Saint-Gaudens. The clack-clackety train took a roundabout route through the sidings and suburbs of Toulouse before heading out up the valley of the river Garonne. A light morning mist hung over the river. Fields of maize stretched across the broad valley floor. Rolling hills rose up on either side. I knew that somewhere up there, in the high hills between Toulouse and the Pyrenees, was my destination: a small village named Péguilhan, where I was going to spend the summer.

The journey to Saint-Gaudens took about fifty minutes. This was as close to Péguilhan as I could get. Only a few people got off the train when it stopped and they soon disappeared. I looked around, my heart full of the excitement of arriving in a new place. I climbed the stone steps up to the old town on the hill. The streets were quiet. I decided to take a breather before heading on to Péguilhan: I needed to get my head together, I hadn't had any breakfast and I was tired and hungry. In the clear blue May morning, I sat on a café terrace with a coffee and a croissant, admiring the panorama of the valley. The sun played with sharp shadows and bright open spaces. I felt the warm air of the South on my face, like a gentle, welcoming caress. Along the terrace the paulownia trees were in full bloom, their pale lilac flowers, hanging in clusters, giving off a distinctive, earthy, musk-rose scent, captivating and evocative of rich smells and tastes.

How was I going to get to Péguilhan? I spread the map out on the table. It was about another thirty or forty kilometres away, in the middle of nowhere. There was no railway line. I asked in the café, but they were rather vague and told me they didn't think there was a bus that could take me there. I walked to the edge of town. There was no one else around to ask. A road sign with a diagonal red line through the name ST-GAUDENS marked the end of the town and the start of open country. The morning was warming up and a heat haze was beginning to shimmer above the tarmac. The road, shaded only by trees spaced at intervals along the verges, stretched out into the distance. This was the last frontier; from here on I was heading into the unknown.

I tried to hitch a lift from a passing car, but when it stopped the driver told me he was only going to the next farm. A tractor driver shrugged his shoulders as he went by, as if to tell me he had no room. After that there was no traffic at all for what seemed like ages. Standing by the empty roadside, the excitement I'd felt earlier was quickly evaporating. I felt a twinge of uncertainty, not knowing what I'd let myself in for. *You can always turn round and go home now*, I thought. I had an open return ticket from Toulouse to back to London. *No, Martin*, I told myself, *you're made of stronger stuff than that*.

I walked back into town, found a phone box and phoned the Auberge to ask if someone could come to meet me. After more than an hour a big white Renault 25 saloon drew up, swung round and stopped in front of me. A tall woman, with dark curly hair and an imposing manner, got out of the driver's seat and came over to me.

'Are you Martin?' she asked me cautiously, in French.

'Yes, that's me,' I replied.

'Ah! Very good,' she said, reassured. 'I'm Marie-Jeanne Cazagnac.'

Her manner changed: she became less serious and much warmer. She shook my hand and asked if I'd had a good journey. Before I could reply, a teenage boy of about 14 got out of the other side of the car and came running round to greet me, beaming with excitement at the new arrival.

'Monsieur Martin! Monsieur Martin!' he cried. I think the repetition was more for his amusement than to confirm who I was.

Marie-Jeanne introduced me to her youngest son, Nicolas, and we shook hands exaggeratedly. Still tired from my journey, I was a little taken aback by the attention.

I was given the new arrival's special privilege of sitting in the front passenger seat, while Nicolas perched in the back, leaning forward between the two front seats, talking excitedly as we went. He kept a running commentary going as he pointed out things along the way.

'Up that road is the farm where we buy our ducks… I go to school over that way… One of my best friends from school lives on that farm…'

We turned up a narrow road. The land rose, then dipped, then rose again towards an undulating plateau.

Nicolas went quiet for a moment, until we passed the sign entering Péguilhan, when he announced proudly: 'Here is our village!'

We drove along the main road through the centre of the village, past the château and the church. There wasn't a soul about. When it seemed we were about to go right through Péguilhan and out the other side, we turned off sharply to the right. Nicolas tapped me heavily on the shoulder.

'It's there, the Auberge,' he said, pointing straight ahead up the hill.

The Auberge stood on high ground, up a narrow drive, above the double hairpin bend in the road into the village from the north. A hand-painted welcome sign stood at the corner of the drive: *BIENVENU À L'AUBERGE*.

It was a solid-looking building, golden-brown stone and render, with an ancient panelled oak door in the centre. Carved into the stone arch above the door was the date 1769. Attached to the wall to the right was an old bell with a rusty chain pull. Symmetrical and simple, with five windows and one door, the front was like a child's drawing of a house. Wooden shutters framed the windows, geraniums tumbled from window boxes and wisteria trailed up the wall. Under a cerulean sky, a low-pitched terracotta-tiled roof evoked long, hot, dry summers. This was a plain country house, squat, with thick walls pressing into the earth. Made from local materials, the building appeared to blend with the land.

A paddock for horses lay to the left of the building and wooded slopes fell away to the sides. A children's swing stood in a clearing in the trees. The hilltop setting was a peaceful oasis. The Auberge looked a happy place to be.

'Wow,' I said, 'this is beautiful.'

The front of the Auberge looked out over the valley. The air was clear, and far in the distance I could see the faint grey and white jagged outline of the mountains.

'The Pyrenees,' Marie-Jeanne confirmed.

We walked up the short flight of steps leading to the front door, into the relative dark and cool of the hall, then down a few steps into the dining room, where I met Jacques-Henri Cazagnac, the *aubergiste*.

'I am a Gascon,' were his first words to me. He grabbed my hand between his big, strong farmer's hands and shook it with robust enthusiasm.

'Welcome to Gascony,' he continued, stepping back and spreading out his arms expansively. A typical Gascon farmer, he was short, stockily built, and a larger-than-life character.

Marie-Jeanne, assuming that an Englishman far away from home would appreciate some tea, offered me some and disappeared into the kitchen.

Jacques-Henri pulled out a chair for me to sit down at the table. I looked around the room. A bow-sided grandfather clock stood in the corner, its heavy pendulum steadily keeping time in the stout, violin-shaped case.

Family photographs were on the mantelpiece, some old black-and-white portraits of people from a bygone age and more recent colour photographs. I recognised Jacques-Henri and Marie-Jeanne, and a younger Nicolas.

Marie-Jeanne reappeared, carrying a tray with a pot of Lipton's lemon tea and a slice of her homemade plum tart. Jacques-Henri hovered attentively to see if I would approve. I thanked them both and said the tea made me feel quite at home. They looked pleased – this was obviously the right thing to say.

When I'd finished my tea I was shown up to my room. The wood of the old staircase was battered and worn; the steps creaked, as if they might give way. Slats hung loose in the banisters. The whole building smelled of old wood.

After I'd changed and unpacked the few belongings I'd thrown into my rucksack when I left home two days before, I came downstairs and Jacques-Henri gave me the pair of turquoise rope-soled espadrilles I was to wear for most of the summer.

'They'll be comfortable,' he said. 'This is what everyone wears here in summer.'

The word espadrille comes from the old southern French dialect word *espardillo*, referring to the rope-soled canvas shoes originally worn in the Pyrenees for clambering over mountain pathways in fine weather.

In the afternoon, Marie-Jeanne showed me round the Auberge. We walked along the gallery round the rear courtyard. The back walls were timber framed, in a vertical-lined structure, which Marie-Jeanne told me they call *torchis et colombage*. The dark brown wooden beams were infilled with sand-coloured plaster. In the courtyard below us, a big rectangular stone table stood on a raised gravel terrace. Marie-Jeanne enjoyed pointing out the flowers growing plentifully in wooden barrels and stone troughs: pelargoniums, fuchsias and marigolds. Climbing roses cascaded over the edge of the terrace. Crimson bougainvillea and multicoloured sweet peas trailed over a trellis set against the wall. The flowers created lively splashes of colour in a landscape that was otherwise shades of golden brown and green. The impression was rustic, a little disorderly, yet lovingly cared for. The windows to the rear of the old stable block gave commanding views over the picturesque valley of the river Gesse. The land immediately behind the building plunged down to a wheatfield far below, where an old shepherd's hut jutted out from the edge of a wood.

We walked out of the roofed gateway back onto the front drive. I looked down towards a very curious-looking construction, the like of which I'd never seen before. Standing beside the drive, it was a sort of open shed consisting of a wooden frame, several metres long and about a metre wide, with chicken-wire walls, a door at one end and a single-pitch tiled roof.

'What's that?' I asked Marie-Jeanne.

'It's a *séchoir*,' she told me. 'They are used for air-drying maize. This one isn't used any more, but come September, you'll see other *séchoirs* in the village stacked full of yellow maize heads.'

I stifled a yawn. I'd been travelling by train and boat for about thirty-six hours. Marie-Jeanne was sympathetic and suggested I go to have a rest in my room before dinner.

In the evening, feeling revived, I met the rest of the family. Paul, the eldest son, was 22. He'd just finished his military service, which he was keen to point out he'd hated. Bruno, the middle son, was 18 and was hoping to go to agricultural college. We all sat down around the stone table on the terrace, where we would eat *en plein air* most evenings. We enjoyed a hearty meal of stewed lamb and rustic red wine.

With everyone talking quickly in the southwest accent, I struggled to follow everything that was being said. I listened closely to try to hear the patterns. They pronounced the normally silent *e* that shouldn't be said, and they also added a twangy *g* to words ending with a nasal vowel. As I listened, I noticed how the accent had an earthiness about it, and a lively, singsong quality.

'*Martaing, tu veux du paing et du vaing?*' Jacques-Henri asked me.

'Huh?' I asked, smiling awkwardly.

He repeated the question. Then he offered me some bread to go with the stew and some more wine. I had to think for a moment. At last, the light dawned. What he was really saying was: '*Martin, tu veux du pain et du vin?*' Martin, do you want some bread and wine?

He laughed cheekily. I suspected he may have been playing up the accent to confuse the foreigner. Now at least I could understand what he was telling me when he said that tomorrow – *demaing* – he would show me around the farm, where I would be starting work.

It was a good first evening. Despite the communication problems, I was made to feel at ease by the warm welcome, the easy-going manner of the family and Jacques-Henri's sense of humour.

My room was at the back of the Auberge. That first night, when all was quiet, I could hear the old building creaking gently as it breathed. I looked out of my small, high window, up towards the cloudless sky. There were no main roads nearby, no streetlamps, few dwellings and no large towns. The night was dark and the stars shone brightly in the heavens, as if some celestial hand had turned up the brightness. There seemed to be more stars than there was sky to hold them. I recognised the W form of the constellation Cassiopeia, shining more brilliantly than I'd ever seen it before. For the first time I experienced the distinctive night-time smell of the countryside in Gascony, a faint odour of burnt earth and sleeping animal.

# EN FAMILLE

THE NEXT MORNING WE HAD BREAKFAST IN THE SMALL FAMILY dining room. Breakfast was a sharp, busy time. The family didn't speak much, concentrating instead on the sugary food and the strong black coffee. Conversation was limited to minimal statements about the work planned for the day, what jobs needed doing, who would go to the farm and who would stay at the Auberge. I couldn't follow what they were talking about – not because of the accent, which by then I was beginning to tune my ear to, but because I had no idea about the work they did or how they ran their farm. All I could do was listen and hope that in time I would understand what was going on. The family didn't pay any special attention to me, as if it were perfectly normal for me to be there.

No sooner had we stacked the coffee bowls in the middle of the table and put the lids back on the jam and honey pots than it was time to go. Marie-Jeanne would clear the table. Jacques-Henri was taking me out to the farm to show me around. I was going to start work today: the welcome period was over.

I was employed as a *stagiaire*, a temporary worker, a sort of trainee general dogsbody with a wide-ranging remit. I was given bed and board and a small allowance, living more or less as part of the family, in return for my work. I was the first *stagiaire* to arrive that summer and the family's first ever English worker.

14

'We're expecting three more *stagiaires* to arrive in the next couple of weeks,' Jacques-Henri told me. 'Another Englishman, a French woman and a German woman. Two of each! We're very traditional here: men do the heavy work outdoors, women do the lighter work indoors. You'll be working at the Auberge some of the time, but you'll be needed most at the farm.'

The farm lay in a deeply secluded location, on a gently sloping hilltop to the east of the village, beyond the back of beyond. A couple of kilometres along the road from Péguilhan to the next village, where the road turned sharp left, a narrow track led straight ahead, along the ridge of a hill, for about a kilometre. The track passed a long, low, ramshackle barn, with crumbling rendered walls, then a smaller barn with a grain loft, before turning into a yard in front of the farmhouse, which was similar in appearance to the Auberge. Next to the house was a small pond, thick with duckweed. A couple of ducks paddled leisurely around, leaving behind them clear channels that slowly closed over as they passed.

A banana tree stood in the centre of the yard. It impressed me with its giant, flat, bright green leaves, and I showed some surprise at seeing it there. Jacques-Henri glowered suspiciously. He didn't know why I was surprised and was ready to take offence. His peasant pride was sensitive to whenever outsiders might be judging him or looking down on him. I told him that where I came from we couldn't grow banana trees outdoors, and that like palm trees, they evoke luxury and the exotic. *C'est l'exotique, quoi*! He was pleased with this account and the moment of tension eased. He explained that the bananas on his tree ripened to yellow but remained small and hard, never growing longer than about ten centimetres. The climate of Gascony was hot enough for them to mature, but not wet enough for them to fill out.

Jacques-Henri showed me some of the work that had to be done on the farm: watering the tomatoes, picking the vegetables, looking after the animals – feeding the cows and shepherding the sheep – and, later in the season, harvesting grain. It was a lot for me to take in at first. This was clearly going to be no holiday.

'I only usually see sheep and cows from the window of a car or a train,' I confessed.

Jacques-Henri shook his head in disbelief, thinking that I had a lot to learn. He may have been wondering just what sort of townie he'd got here. I said I thought I could cope. He told me I had to adapt – *il faut s'adapter*!

He set me to one of the simplest jobs on the farm: watering the tomatoes. The tomato plants stood on an inclined field near the farmhouse. Jacques-Henri pointed to the striped green hosepipe connected to a tap on the outside wall of the farmhouse.

'Give them plenty of water,' he said. 'They're always thirsty!' Then having told me what to do, he left me to my own devices.

I walked up and down the rows, dragging the hosepipe carefully between the plants. The pipe didn't have a nozzle. I squeezed the open end between my thumb and forefinger, splattering water around the stems of several thirsty vines at once. I took off my new espadrilles so they wouldn't get muddy. The field was on a slight incline, an advantage I exploited, creating channels with my bare feet, directing the water in rivulets around the stems of the tomato plants. This minimised the water loss and seemed to get the job done in a shorter time. I enjoyed feeling the cool water run over my feet. I squeezed the light brown mud with my toes, creating small pools that whirled around as the fresh water ran over the top. All the while I tried not to touch the plants. I loathe the smell of tomato leaves and I cannot connect the taste of a warm, fresh tomato with the pungent, cat-like smell of its vine.

Jacques-Henri had made a point of leaving me on my own, but all the while he discreetly kept an eye on me from whatever he was doing.

I must have passed the first test. Jacques-Henri didn't say so, but in the car as we drove back to the Auberge for lunch he was much more matey. He had never been to England; in fact his one and only trip abroad had been over the mountains to Spain. He knew just three expressions in English: *how do you do*, *gentleman-farmer* and *Duke of Wellington*. The name Wellington was absurdly difficult for him to pronounce: *Veh-leng-teng*.

Back at the Auberge, Jacques-Henri asked me if I wanted a *crêpe*.

'Yes, I'd like a *crêpe*,' I replied, politely. I was a little unsure where this was going.

Three times he asked me the same, just to make sure.

He then demonstrated for me that *crêpe* was a slang word for a slap in the face. He roared with laughter – at least he thought it was funny – and walked off chuckling to himself. I wouldn't be caught out like that again.

No matter what was happening, mealtimes were the focal point to which we would always return, three times a day, to sit together as a family. Marie-Jeanne would call us to table – *tout le monde à table*! We weren't fooled by the kindly tone of her voice: there was clearly an iron will behind the velvet tones. Nobody disobeyed her. Mealtimes were a sort of family muster station, where we assembled to take stock of what was going on and to see how everyone was, before dispersing again to the wide range of daily tasks.

It was back to the farm for the afternoon. Paul went off to tend to the sheep, Bruno to feed and water the cattle. Jacques-Henri and I dragged a big piece of agricultural machinery called a *cultivateur* out of the barn into the yard. He explained what it did: like a rotating plough, it attached to the back of the tractor and was used for breaking up the soil. The attachment mechanism had to be taken apart and cleaned. All I could do was watch and pass the tools as Jacques-Henri needed them. I didn't know what all the tools and components were called, so he pointed and explained when I wasn't sure. For me this was a completely new way of living and working and I was learning about farm work from first principles. If I hadn't already spoken good French before I went to Gascony, I simply wouldn't have been able to survive in this environment, where no one spoke English.

Before returning to the Auberge for dinner, I was told to water the tomatoes again. This was my first full day and my second tomato-watering duty!

Tomato watering would be one of my regular jobs. The plants were very heavily fruiting and needed copious amounts of water, so they had to be drenched twice a day, morning and evening. Occasionally I picked a tomato; they were good enough to eat like apples.

At dinner, I saw not just the practical side of mealtimes – planning the day's work and reporting what was going on – but also the deeper meaning of the family table.

Sitting together, *en famille*, sharing their good country food, swapping stories, listening to the sounds of familiar voices, this was a ritual that affirmed the bonds holding the family together. Cazagnac was a local name. Family names and place names in southwest France ending with –ac are derived from the old dialect word for a domain. The family had farmed in the area for generations.

Jacques-Henri rhapsodised over the pleasures of the table. He was most enthusiastic about the quality of the meat from the animals they reared on the farm. For him meat represented prosperity and wellbeing and was something to be shared. It was an insult to the host if a guest did not gladly accept the meat offered. He relished telling me how meat should be eaten to the bone, where the tastiest and most nutritious parts are to be found.

'The meat on the bone is most *savoureuse*,' he said, warming to his theme, tapping his lips with his fingers and thumb.

Lamb was his favourite. When he was enjoying a good gigot of lamb he would hold the gigot with his fingers and hungrily pick off every last morsel of flesh.

'Put down your knife and fork,' he told me. 'Pick up the lamb by the bone and get stuck in!'

Over dinner, Jacques-Henri and Marie-Jeanne told me how they'd come to open the Auberge.

'I inherited the place from my Uncle Guillaume, when he passed away ten years ago,' Marie-Jeanne said. 'It was in a sorry state! Cobwebs hung thick from the ceiling. The grandfather clock in the dining room had stopped years before, and a family of mice was nesting in the base. Uncle Guillaume had loved living here, but in his old age he'd let the place go.'

19

'The outbuildings were in a worse state than the main house,' added Jacques-Henri. 'The back field was overgrown with teasels and thistles. *Dieu vivant*! You can imagine how shameful this looked to a farmer like me.'

'We were very fortunate,' Marie-Jeanne went on. 'Although it was neglected, we could see the potential. We didn't do much at first, Nicolas was young and we were very busy.'

'We worked on the building through several consecutive winters, when things were slack at the farm,' Jacques-Henri explained.

'We had the grandfather clock repaired,' added Marie-Jeanne. 'The clockmaker said it was a real *objet de famille*.'

'Bit by bit, things started to take shape,' Jacques-Henri continued. 'The most important moment for us was when we put up the welcome sign by the drive: *BIENVENU À L'AUBERGE*. Our first guests arrived soon afterwards. That was last spring. *Et nous voilà maintenant*!' And now here we are.

They had spotted the potential of combining the convenience of an inn, situated close to the village, with the produce of their own farm. The Auberge and the farm formed an almost self-sufficient unit: the produce of the farm supplied the Auberge, any surplus was sold, and the income from both supported the whole system. The family worked well as a team. The fact that they were now employing *stagiaires* for the summer showed that the business was becoming a success.

The Auberge was enjoying a new lease of life thanks to their efforts. It showed visitors modern life in the country and the memory of farming life as it used to be. It was not just about making a living, it was also about maintaining a way of life. The farm could barely pay for itself on its own, and the extra income from the Auberge was necessary to maintain the family. There were three sons growing up, who would one day want to start families of their own. Opening the Auberge, although perhaps risky, would hopefully ensure that all the land stayed in the family. As Jacques-Henri had already told me, *il faut s'adapter*, and adapting to economic necessity was just what this family had learned to do.

The word *auberge* comes from the old dialect word *alberga*, meaning lodging. *Auberges*, or country inns, were opened first by abbeys in the Middle Ages. Many were set up along the pilgrim routes through southern France. Guests shared their table and accommodation with other travellers. Nowadays, communal eating and sleeping are no longer expected of visitors, but a good *auberge* should retain something of the original simplicity and should serve hearty country food.

The Cazagnac family Auberge catered for different appetites, from a simple *assiette gasconne* of salad topped with cold meat in the form of *jambon de bayonne* and *gésiers de canard*, to more convivial feasts of grilled duck breast, stuffed shoulder of lamb and *cassoulet*. Bed-and-breakfast accommodation was offered in *chambres d'hôte*. The rooms had beamed ceilings, beam and plaster walls and well-worn oak floorboards. Old-fashioned candlewick bedspreads covered the wide, rickety beds. Citrus and clove-scented pomanders hung from the keys in the doors of the big old wardrobes. There were no televisions or radios; in fact, there was little sign at all of the outside world. The rooms were individually named: *Charme*,

*Chouette*, *Treille*… Charm, Owl, Vine. An antique wooden cot stood on the landing and was carried into the room for the very youngest guests.

The old stable block and hayloft around the rear of the courtyard had been renovated, the upstairs converted into five *gîtes* and the downstairs into a function room for wedding receptions and country feasts. The refurbishment was nearly complete. The builders had done most of the work, and all that was left was some decorating and finishing off. Three *gîtes* were in a fit state to be let out, and Jacques-Henri hoped the other two would be ready by the end of the summer.

The Auberge gave visitors a feeling of being deep in the countryside and was a haven for people seeking peace and seclusion. Some visitors had special reasons for coming to an extremely out-of-the-way place, where they wouldn't be seen. One afternoon, a few days after I arrived, two Dutch couples rolled up in a big black BMW. The car looked menacing, and sounded it too, as its wide tyres crunched the gravel. The occupants were of a certain age and looked very serious. Appearances were deceiving: it turned out they were naturists. Jacques-Henri warned me discreetly when they were out in the far field, as he put it *à poile*, sunbathing and frolicking in the altogether, so fortunately I never saw them *au naturel* with my own eyes!

# THE GENIAL HOST

I ENJOYED MY BREAKFASTS: CHUNKY TARTINES OF BREAD, THICKLY covered with butter, jam, honey and Nutella chocolate spread, not necessarily all at once. I loved working the honey into the butter on a slice of bread to form a smooth, sweet paste, then letting it melt on my tongue, the sweetness so intense it would sting.

There were no alarm clocks: we woke up naturally, and it was expected that everyone would be at the breakfast table by 7.30 sharp. We had lunch at midday and dinner at six in the evening. The routine of family mealtimes was as certain as the permanent sunshine and the age-old rhythms of the countryside. There was a strict logic in how we ate and drank. Breakfast was sugary and sweet, to give us the energy for a hard day's labour, with big bowls of strong coffee to wake us up. Lunch was usually the heaviest meal of the day. This was the end of May, so the summer was just warming up, but come July and August, when the midday air was too hot and the sun too fierce for us to work inside or out, we would have a siesta after lunch, *faire la sieste*. Afterwards, to perk ourselves up, we reheated the coffee left over from the morning.

In the early evening, before the restaurant opened, we ate dinner sitting around the stone table in the courtyard. This was a good time of day, when the heat of the afternoon was just beginning to subside into a comfortable evening warmth. Everyone chatted easily and the tone was always warm and optimistic. Dinner was usually a light meal, so we remained lively through the evening. We never had coffee in the evening, and we drank enough wine to enjoy a little and help digest our meal. The pattern of consumption was perfectly suited to the working rhythms of the day and the need for a solid night's sleep.

As I grew accustomed to my new surroundings, I could see how every aspect of life knitted together, and how everyone had their role to play. Jacques-Henri fitted perfectly the character of the genial host, always ready to welcome people to his hostelry and give them an authentic taste of the country. The visitors who came were mostly Dutch and German, in search of escape and tranquillity in this isolated spot. Jacques-Henri was interested in meeting people from different countries and he seemed to get on with them all, no matter where they came from or whether or not he could understand a word they were saying. Whenever he thought he was being complimented on his hospitality, he would swell with pride and laugh with satisfaction.

Jacques-Henri was entertaining, sometimes high-spirited, and sometimes obstinate and irreverent. I was occasionally unsure when he was being serious and when he was joking. He had a roguish twinkle in his eye and his head had a slight forward tilt, giving the impression he was about to do something mischievous. His mischief was usually little more than poking fun at people he liked, always done with good humour.

The twinkle in Jacques-Henri's eye was enlivened by secret slugs of Armagnac, which he drank by sidling off into a corner of the room and raising his arm in line with the bottle, in an attempt at concealing it while he took a draught. He would glance around guiltily afterwards to see if anyone had noticed, but everyone ignored him.

Marie-Jeanne and Jacques-Henri were very different from each other. Marie-Jeanne was a strong, silent presence. She was taller than her husband, big framed but quite slim. She had a kindly smile and was always simply dressed. Her cooking invariably appeared on the table on time, with what looked like effortless ease. She was a woman of determination and good sense.

Marie-Jeanne was often relieved when Jacques-Henri went off to 'play', as she put it, at the farm, leaving her to manage the business her way. She was in charge at the Auberge, he ran the farm. Her business head complemented his knowledge of farming and his *joie de vivre*. When Marie-Jeanne complained that Jacques-Henri should do a little less jollification and a little more work in the kitchen, he went quietly outside to smoke a cigar.

The three sons, Paul, Bruno and Nicolas, were also very different from each other. Paul was easy-going. Bruno took his work at the farm and the Auberge very seriously. He was practical, and like his mother he didn't talk a lot. Nicolas, bless him, the youngest, *le petit dernier*, was a natural clown who didn't take anything very seriously at all. He rode his Peugeot *mobylette* every day to the school in the nearest town, Boulogne-sur-Gesse, seven kilometres away. Out of school hours and during the long holidays he worked around the Auberge and the farm, but made a mess of everything he attempted. Paul was protective of his little brother and he frequently remarked, with an ironic roll of the eyes, that with Nicolas it was nothing but cock-ups. *Que des conneries!* Nicolas's clowning around was probably due to his age; his mind was always somewhere else. I think Paul took after his father, Bruno took after his mother, and I'm not sure which parent Nicolas resembled.

The Cazagnacs were, it seemed, the most hospitable Gascon family you could hope to meet, with a strong sense of belonging to their land and yet open to welcoming visitors. Jacques-Henri only had one *bête noire*, a chink in his armour of geniality: Parisians! A Parisian couple came to stay at the Auberge. The number plate on their car ending with 75 for Paris signalled trouble as they drew up. The man in the driver's seat had a haughty, disdainful look about him. The woman, elegantly dressed, got out and opened a back door of the car. The air of attentiveness and pride in her manner led us to expect her to bring out a small, well-dressed child, but instead out jumped an elaborately clipped white poodle wearing a sparkling diamanté collar. This was going too far!

'They come down here with their fancy poodles,' muttered Jacques-Henri under his breath. 'How would they like it if I went for a walk down the Champs-Élysées with a sheep?'

*Jacques-Henri*

# MAIGRET OR MAGRET?

I HAD TO LEARN TO DRIVE THE CITROËN 2CV VAN, SO THAT I could shuttle backwards and forwards between the Auberge and the farm as and when I was needed. Just because I could drive a car didn't mean I could drive a 2CV.

The Cazagnac's battered old cream-coloured van with corrugated side panels, known as *une fourgonnette*, had seen a lot of service and really shouldn't have been on the road. The handbrake didn't work, so when it was parked, to stop it from rolling away it had to be driven up against a wall, a wooden block or a bank of earth. This hardly mattered: the bumper was already bent and one of the front headlamps was twisted downwards, so that from the front the van looked like a battered featherweight boxer trying to wink. A bash to the hinges on the driver's door had wedged it permanently shut, so we had to climb in and out of the passenger side. The door windows on all 2CVs fold outwards and upwards, as anyone familiar with the vehicle knows. The window catches on the Cazagnac's van were broken, so when it went round corners or over bumps the windows flew out like an elephant's ears.

Paul gave me a driving lesson. The gear lever was a handle below the dashboard that had to be pushed and pulled and twisted, like an uncooperative umbrella handle with a car attached. The rest of the controls were minimal. The flap below the windscreen opened for air-conditioning;

a mesh strained out the insects, highly effectively judging by the number of dead flies stuck in it.

I started the 2CV and thrashed it up through the gears to top gear as quickly as possible, which was the only way to get it to pick up any speed. The engine chugged uncomfortably for some distance before it found its rhythm. What was frustrating was that it seemed to go at just one speed – slow – whether I pressed the accelerator lightly or floored it. I leant forward, willing it to go just a little faster, but it didn't take any notice of me.

The popular myth about the Citroën 2CV is that it was originally designed to carry two peasants and a basket of eggs across a bumpy field without breaking any of either. The soft suspension meant that on winding roads it rolled all over the place, and when it came to a sudden stop it bobbed about like a drunken Space Hopper.

This underpowered glorified eggbox on wheels had real difficulty with steep hills. Midway between Péguilhan and the farm there was a steep dip and a bend in the road. The only way to get the van up the hill was to fling it down into the bend as fast as possible – it leant over at a truly alarming angle, seeming as if it might topple over – and use the excess speed to carry it up the hill. It was great fun as the van slewed into the bend, tilting sideways, then climbed the hill, going slower and slower, until it had almost stopped as it reached the top and the engine caught up with it again.

I'd only just got the hang of this reckless manoeuvre when hurtling out of the bend, with Paul in the passenger seat, we met an oncoming herd of cows. I slammed on the brakes and we screeched to a halt, just a couple of metres from the lead animals. The 2CV lurched forward on its soft springs as it came to a stop. We weren't wearing seat-belts. I held on to the steering wheel as firmly as I could; Paul pressed his hands on the dashboard. Then we slumped back in our seats. Paul gave an *ouf* of relief. *Merde*, that was close. I was stunned. The cows in front of the van stood stock-still and looked at us, unperturbed, hardly blinking a long-lashed eyelid in the face of the danger they'd so narrowly escaped. We had to sit and wait until they'd all ambled slowly by, in their own time. One of them mooed deeply as it passed, I think to remind us this was their bit of road.

I stretched my arm out of the window to touch a cow that was passing close on my side. Paul warned me not to.

'Don't touch,' he said, with matter-of-fact severity. 'If it kicks the van its hoof will go right through the door panel.'

The farmer brought up the rear of the herd. He was old and wiry, but with a spring in his step. He wore tradi-tional blue work overalls and a beret, and was carrying a long stick to herd the cows. Recognising Paul he grinned at us, then with a friendly gesture rapped his stick on the bonnet of the van, just as he would thwack a cow on the rump.

'*Salut, les gars!*' he shouted. Hello guys.

'*Salut!*' Paul shouted in return, then as soon as the old farmer was out of earshot, added '*Et merci!*' sarcastically.

We set off again, arriving safely at the farm where we set about the different tasks that needed attention – sheep, cows, machinery, watering – and then returned to the Auberge in the afternoon.

That evening I was given a new test: cooking. Not just for the family, but for guests in the restaurant. I enjoy cooking, but I knew nothing about traditional fare in Gascony.

Marie-Jeanne told me I was going to cook *magrets* on the outdoor grill. At first I thought she was talking about Inspector Maigret, the fictional detective character.

'No, not Maigret, *magret*. It's one of our specialities here, *magret de canard*,' Marie-Jeanne explained, slightly amused.

A *magret de canard*, as we prepared it *à la* Cazagnac, was a breast of duck scored in a criss-cross pattern on the fatty side, grilled in a wire cage over a wood-burning grill set in an alcove in the stone wall of the courtyard. I must have passed the first test well, because I went on to cook a lot of *magrets* that summer – I can't even guess how many, but it was a lot! It was my most elevated culinary duty. During the high season in July and August, I cooked *magrets* almost every evening.

When the restaurant was expected to be busy, I had to set the wood burning a couple of hours before we opened, so it would be reduced to glowing charcoal when it was time to start grilling. I cooked the fleshy side first, to allow the fat to seep into the meat from above. The duck sizzled as the fat dripped, spitting and spattering, into the smoking embers. The smell was always tantalising and the smoke gave a rich, woody flavour to the meat, but I frequently had to step back from the alcove, coughing, to breathe in the open courtyard. It was dirty work, what with the smoke, the ash and the hot grill cage becoming encrusted with fat, yet miraculously the *magrets* remained pure and glistening in the middle of it all.

There were different degrees of grilling a *magret de canard*. The first was *une cuisson bleue*: just cooked on the outside and quite raw inside. The second degree was *rosé*: cooked a little more but still quite pink. The most popular choice at the Auberge was *à point*, medium rare. A *magret* could also be well done, *bien croustillant*, nice and crisp – the way I preferred it.

The guests really appreciated their food, so I had to be sure the *magrets* were done to perfection. With two or three on the go at once, each being grilled to a different degree, I quickly had to get to grips with the mental alertness required for restaurant work.

There would be a shout from the kitchen: 'Is that *magret* ready yet?'

'Which one?' I would shout back.

'The *à point*.'

'Nearly.'

'Good. We need two more, one *rosé*, the other *à point*.'

When the *magrets* were ready, I leant round the kitchen door to pass them to Marie-Jeanne, who finished them off with a sauce. Creamy garlic was the basic sauce, but rich, tangy cherry was a better accompaniment, the sharpness of the fruit cutting through the fattiness of the duck.

*Séchoir*

31

# NEW ARRIVALS

I SPENT THE MORNING PAINTING THE GÎTES IN THE CONVERTED stables behind the Auberge. Farm work may have been new to me, but I'd always helped my parents painting when was growing up, and I was a dab hand, as my father put it, with a paintbrush or a hammer. It was a Saturday and Nicolas was off school. He was 'helping' me. I'd rather he hadn't. If he wasn't wobbling the stepladder while I was standing near the top, he was drawing rude pictures on the bare walls before I painted over them. He still insisted on calling me *Monsieur Martin*. I saw what Paul meant about his little brother: *Que des conneries*! I was relieved when Marie-Jeanne came and called Nicolas to go to the station with her. Nicolas put down his paintbrush in mid-composition and left excitedly to meet the new *stagiaire* at Saint-Gaudens, just as they'd done for me.

I'd been at the Auberge for nearly a fortnight. I was looking forward to another *stagiaire* arriving. I would no longer be the only stranger.

Florence was French and came from a farm up north in the Loire Valley, near Tours. She was always impeccably polite. We did the correct double kiss – *la bise* – when we were introduced. She was 22, dark-haired, gamine, almond-eyed, quite Gallic looking. In the Loire Valley they speak 'proper' French and Florence's accent was much clearer than the Cazagnacs'. I wondered why she'd come to work on a farm in the southwest when she already lived on a farm. This certainly wasn't going to be an new experience for her. I thought she'd either come to get ideas about turning a farm into a more profitable concern, or else – and this seemed more likely – she'd come to find a farmer husband.

Florence immediately took charge of some tasks in the kitchen.

'*Elle a l'air d'être bien dans sa peau ici*,' Marie-Jeanne remarked. She seems very much at ease with herself here. Marie-Jeanne was pleased to have female help around the Auberge, living as she did in a family of men.

David was the next *stagiaire* to arrive, the day after Florence. Marie-Jeanne and Nicolas collected him from the station. He walked into the dining room, a thin, gawky Englishman, looking bemused and surprised to find himself there. He shook hands with everyone, or rather everyone shook hands with him; he was very standoffish. His French was quite dodgy.

At dinner on his first evening, we asked David questions about himself. He said he was going to read philosophy at Cambridge in the autumn. He was very serious and bookish. He wore a black polo-neck sweater, even in the summer heat.

In his poor French, David said he wanted to talk about contemporary French intellectual currents, poststructuralism or something. This was *not* the place!

Jacques-Henri scowled. '*Bof*! Intellectuals,' he said, looking around the table. 'For all their clever ideas,' he asked, 'can they tell me why the shell of one species of snail spirals one way and the shell of another species spirals the other way?'

Then, without waiting for an answer, he made a dismissive puff with his top lip and smiled at the fundamental truth of what he'd just said.

David looked taken aback.

'This isn't a pavement café in Paris, you know,' Jacques-Henri reminded him. And with that, he took down a big green book from the shelf, *Encyclopédie de la Nature*, and plonked it on the table. 'This is all the book learning you need,' he said.

David was painfully out of place at the Auberge. When things were being explained to him he stroked his chin carefully, as if to help stimulate his thought processes.

Mealtimes with David were bizarrely entertaining. The Cazagnacs, like other southern French families, ate all the courses of their meal from the same plate, wiping it clean with a hunk of bread between dishes. Picture the sequence at dinner. We would have a plate of *potage*, thick vegetable soup with small pieces of duck. We sopped up the soup with bread. Then we might have a slice of tart, with salad and peppery green Puy lentils. We cleaned our plates again with bread. Finally, as the culmination of the meal, we ate our gigot of lamb.

Jacques-Henri told David from the start to eat up and wipe his plate clean with a piece of bread. David stroked his chin and nodded, but whether he understood was another matter.

David did not enjoy his food, he just picked at whatever was on his plate. He didn't finish his soup, he left a piece of bread floating in it; put his slice of tart and lentils in the soup, so that the tart went soggy; and then he balanced the gigot of lamb on top of it all. We watched silently, in disbelief, as the food piled up and mixed together on his plate. David prodded the heap disinterestedly with his fork.

He seemed oblivious to what was going on around him, and he'd no idea even of the performance he was giving at mealtimes.

Jacques-Henri just shrugged his shoulders at the English eccentric, more deserving of pity than contempt, and carried on tucking into his gigot of lamb with gusto.

The German *stagiaire* was the last to arrive. Marie-Jeanne and Nicolas had gone to collect her at the station. Brushing the floor in the dining room, I heard the car draw up outside. The shutters on the front window were closed in the midday heat. The new arrival walked down the steps from the front door. The sunlight streaming through the doorway behind her shone like an aura through her pale gold shoulder-length hair. She was wearing a red top with white polka dots and little puff sleeves, her blue jeans turned up at the ankles and carrying a pink canvas rucksack. At first her face was in shadow against the light, then as she stepped down into the room I saw her features clearly. Her eyes were a striking clear blue. She looked around her with an air of hesitant curiosity, her manner sure and calm. She leant forward to put down her rucksack, which had a little toy Babar the Elephant dangling from the front buckle.

Marie-Jeanne did the introductions.

'Anja… Martin,' she said, gesturing with her hands.

'*Enchanté!*'

'*Moi aussi!*' Me too.

She was absolutely gorgeous. *Coup de foudre*. My summer at the Auberge suddenly looked very different.

'Anja's a student at Heidelberg,' said Marie-Jeanne, quite impressed.

'What do you study there?' I asked her.

35

'Languages.'

'Me too!'

Anja spoke good English and even better French. We were destined always to speak to one another in French. We'd both come to the Auberge for a real Gallic experience, as we put it *to live in French*, and it was natural for us to use that as our lingua franca. In truth, I think Anja's French was better than mine.

Marie-Jeanne went into the kitchen to start making coffee for Anja. Nicolas straightened some chairs. I heard Paul out in the courtyard calling me; he needed a second pair of hands to carry the stepladder upstairs.

'*À plus*,' I said to Anja. See you later.

'*À plus*,' she replied.

And I went outside to help Paul with the stepladder.

The arrival of Florence and Anja meant that I would be doing less work around the kitchen and more outdoors at the farm. Florence was a natural in the kitchen, although some of the cooking here in the southwest was different to what she knew in Touraine. Anja was very personable and she would work mainly front of house, waiting on the tables in the restaurant. Marie-Jeanne showed her the order of laying the covers. It was not clear what sort of work David would be suitable for.

# MORE GEESE THAN PEOPLE

FLORENCE, DAVID AND ANJA WERE EACH GIVEN A SMALL ROOM below the *gîtes* to the rear of the Auberge. So far I'd been enjoying the privilege of staying in one of the main upstairs rooms in the Auberge, but this special treatment was not to last. With four *stagiaires* in place and more guests arriving to fill up the accommodation, I was moved off to the farm.

My life with the Cazagnacs entered a new phase. I was given the annex at the back of the farmhouse, a converted outbuilding adjacent to the house. It was a large, simple room, with a tiled floor and a small window looking out on the woods. A small room off to the side had basic washing facilities.

On my first morning at the annex, very early, I stepped outside and breathed in the fresh, sappy smell of the woods. The dew glistened in the morning sunlight shining through the trees. All around me, I could hear the cheerful sounds of a summer day beginning. I felt as though I'd come to a land where time had stood still.

The farm was so isolated the Cazagnacs never bothered to lock the doors to the farmhouse during the day, although often no one was there for hours at a time. The farmhouse and the area around it had an air of neglect, as the family's energies were being channelled into making a success of the Auberge. The farm was their home, and although the whole family still slept there, it was little used. During the summer season the farmhouse's main rooms were hardly ever used. The wooden shutters on the windows looked shabby and were nearly always closed. A few pots by the front door bearing flowers were overgrown, and the dusty edges of the drive were merging with the tufty grass. Long grass was growing through a rusty old plough next to the front door. I think Marie-Jeanne would have liked to do something about this neglect, but neither she nor the rest of the family had the time.

Although the farmhouse may have been neglected, the farmland was well cared for. There was a well-kept kitchen garden behind the main buildings, providing vegetables and herbs. Farther down the slope stood an orchard of plum trees. The farm was surrounded by several hundred acres of wheatfields, a broad field of sunflowers, and open rolling pasture for sheep and cattle. The earth around the farm was a light grey-brown crumbly clay, a blond soil, with a hint of gold, reflecting the rays of the sun. Dense woods covered the slopes beyond the fields, and a small lake, which drained into the river Arjo, lay hidden in the valley to the south.

Standing in front of the farmhouse scanning the landscape, I could not see another house in any direction. The nearest neighbours lived in the farm on the northern side of the valley, tucked in a fold of the land, out of sight behind a copse. The first time I saw the neighbours was from a distance; they were driving cows along the track leading to their farm. The farmer was at the wheel of a blue van behind the cows, hooting his horn repeatedly, while various other members of the family ran around waving sticks and shouting 'Allez! Allez!' The bewildered cows bellowed angrily in return, creating a cacophony of noise that resounded back and forth across the valley.

'The whole family is completely mad,' Jacques-Henri told me dismissively, as if they were not worth talking about. He waved his forefinger in a circular motion at his temple.

The Auberge and the farm were two separate spheres, each with its own atmosphere and tempo. The pace at the Auberge was sometimes frenetic, driven by the constant demands of catering for the guests. The slower rhythm of life at the farm was set by the routines of looking after the animals and growing the crops.

One day, driving to the farm with Jacques-Henri in the 2CV, I smelled an acrid stench coming from a barn near the road.

'What's that smell?' I asked.

'*Caca d'oie*,' he replied. Goose shit.

We were downwind of the goose farm just outside the village. A handmade sign beside the track leading to the goose farm advertised *FOIE GRAS – VENTE DIRECTE*, with a picture of a happy, smiling goose raising a welcoming wing. Poor deluded creature!

We passed a long, low barn, behind a hedge. I saw geese inside and I heard some squawking.

'Did you know that here in Gascony,' Jacques-Henri asked me, 'there are more geese than people? And we Gascons are very independent,' he added. 'Scratch a Gascon and just below the surface you'll find someone who is very proud to be different from the rest of the French. We have our own language, *le parler Gascon*. My mother's first language was Gascon, although I don't remember much now.'

Jacques-Henri referred to the old tongue not so much as a language, but rather as the Gascon way of speaking. There were once so many local dialects, so many pronunciations, that the people from one village often had difficulty understanding those from the next.

We drew up outside the farmhouse and got out of the van.

'Do you know what is the real symbol of being a Gascon?' Jacques-Henri asked me.

'Er, no,' I replied.

'The beret!'

'Oh yes?'

'Wait there,' he said, and disappeared inside the farmhouse, returning a couple of minutes later twirling a beret on his forefinger, which he then flicked onto his head.

'Gascony is the true home of the beret,' Jacques-Henri explained. 'A beret is a shepherd's hat. No one knows exactly where berets were first worn, in the Béarn, in the Basque Country or in the Landes. What is for sure is that the beret is a symbol of our independence here in the southwest. The rest of the French, they copied us.'

Wearing his beret, he looked like a caricature of a rugged Gascon farmer.

His Gascon beret was wider and flatter than a normal beret. Plonked on top of his head, it looked floppy around the edges. The floppiness was what made it so distinctive.

Jacques-Henri leant forward and pointed at the top of his beret. 'The little finger of felt sticking up on top is called a *cabilhou*, which means wooden peg,' he told me. 'It's there to ward off bad luck.'

Jacques-Henri loved his farm. He preferred being there to being at the Auberge, because however entertaining he was in the role of the *aubergiste*, the farm was the place he felt he really belonged.

I sometimes accompanied him on his evening tour around various outlying parts of the farm. He told me things about the land and how it was managed. He liked to watch the close of the day, he said, because no two were ever the same. He breathed in the warm evening air, looked around him, admiring the countryside, and said, '*Ah, la campagne! Tout est à sa place.*' Everything is in its place.

Jacques-Henri believed that living off the land was not just something you did, but a privilege. He said it was about putting back in what you took out. He spoke of the land as a living being. He made it clear in no uncertain terms that he objected to paying taxes to the government in Paris. The *ministres*, he said, did not represent him at all.

'They think we're just *ploucs* down here.'

'*Ploucs?*' I enquired.

'Yes, simple people who live in the country,' he explained.

'Oh, I see.' Bumpkins.

He looked at me sternly, to make sure I did *not* agree.

One evening, we stomped down towards the fresh, tall grass at the bottom of the dry valley. Jacques-Henri told me a lot of vipers had their nests here. The warm evening air whispered through the long grass. I imagined the snakes slithering silently along, listening to our footsteps with their bodies flattened against the earth, their tiny forked tongues darting in and out, testing the air.

'Don't worry,' Jacques-Henri said, 'they're only active in the heat of the day, they shouldn't bite you.'

'Well, just so long as they know that,' I said.

41

Standing there in my baggy canvas shorts and flimsy espadrilles, I looked around, hoping the vipers would not be out late that evening.

Through Jacques-Henri, I was beginning to see the sense of obligation that tied a Gascon farmer to his land. Being a true farmer was about understanding the balance between owning the land and belonging to it in turn, taking the time to read the barely noticeable messages the land and the animals were giving out, and knowing how to respond.

# MELON-SEED NECKLACE

**N**OW THAT I WAS SLEEPING AT THE FARM, ALONG WITH THE family I had to make the journey to the Auberge each morning for breakfast. Marie-Jeanne would often go ahead in the Renault, sometimes Jacques-Henri went with her, and the rest of us – too many for comfort – crammed ourselves into the 2CV van.

On the daily early-morning drive from the farm to the Auberge, the sun would be climbing in the sky above faraway hills, and I would be starting to think about breakfast. I was getting used to the idea that every day would be fine and sunny. Each morning as we turned up the road into Péguilhan, I heard a cockerel crowing somewhere in the village, making everyone aware of his presence, announcing the start of a new day, sometimes quite persistently. I heard the strident call so many times, but from the sound alone I couldn't locate him. One morning I tracked him down to a farmyard on the far side of the village, strutting his stuff in front of the henhouse.

On weekday mornings when Nicolas was going to school, he rode his *mobylette* in front of us, weaving his way through an imaginary slalom course, his head thrust forward, pretending he was a superbike racer.

Monday was the one day a week when we took things relatively easy. The restaurant was closed on Monday lunchtimes, and so on those mornings, although some work had to go on at the farm, the Auberge was quiet. On the first Monday we were all together, after breakfast all the younger members of the team – me, Anja, Florence, David, the brothers Paul and Bruno; Nicolas was at school – sat around the stone table on the terrace in the sunlit courtyard for a long-drawn-out coffee.

We were just getting to know each other. David was reading a serious-looking book with a plain black cover. Anja was reading a novel by George Sand. I was flicking through a farming magazine. Bruno brought out a stack of wooden vegetable storage trays and set about repairing the broken ones. Paul was in the kitchen making coffee.

Florence was doing something curious. Since she'd arrived, she'd scooped out, washed and saved the seeds from all the melons we'd eaten. Now, she spread them out on the table, took a long piece of black twine, threaded it on a needle and began to poke the needle through the flat side of the seeds one after another, sliding them down the twine like beads. She was concentrating very hard, following the movements of the needle with her tongue around the corners of her mouth.

When she'd finished, she pushed the seeds tightly together, straightened them, tied up the ends of the cotton, and held up her melon-seed necklace. It was about fifty or sixty centimetres long. Halfway along she tied a small loop, which hung in the shape of a teardrop. She looked pleased with her work and put the handmade jewellery round her neck. The necklace looked primitive, and I thought it made her look like a cave-girl. I guessed this sort of simple craft was something she'd learned to do as a child on a farm.

As Florence put on her creation, Paul came out of the kitchen with a fresh saucepan of coffee for everyone. He said that the necklace made her look very pretty. Florence blushed. Paul went round refilling our bowls with fresh coffee.

David came to an interesting part of his book. 'Hum,' he said to himself, meaningfully, and stroked his chin.

Anja smiled at this, and bit her lip as she tried not to giggle.

Bruno got a splinter stuck in his hand from a broken tray. He whispered an unrepeatable French expletive, then looked up at everyone and apologised.

I was losing interest in the farming magazine. Enough about combine harvesters, hay baling and the problems facing goatherds at this time of year.

I turned to Anja. 'Why are you studying languages?' I asked.

'I'm curious about the world,' she explained. 'I like meeting people from different cultures.'

'What do you think you'll do with your languages?'

'I don't know, I'm only just 20!'

Paul and Florence were talking about what it had been like for each of them growing up on their respective farms.

'*Chez nous…*' I just caught Florence saying.

'*…et moi aussi,*' Paul answered.

Bruno interrupted us all. '*Il faut aller bosser maintenant,*' he announced. Back to the grind; some work would have to be done before lunch.

Bruno cleared away the coffee bowls and we all went to our tasks. We knew our roles by now – except David, who stood around, looking aloof.

I don't know whether David was really unable, or just unwilling, to join in with the work. It was clear that he had no practical sense at all. Jacques-Henri thought he'd better give him something simple to do, so he asked him to sweep the staircase leading up to the gallery. He handed David the broom and left him to it.

A few minutes later, while I was working in the ground-floor *gîte*, Bruno came to speak to me. 'Come quickly and see what David's doing,' he whispered conspiratorially.

I followed Bruno out to the courtyard, where Jacques-Henri and Paul were watching David sweep the gallery staircase.

Instead of using his common sense, starting at the top and sweeping the dust down from step to step, David had begun at the bottom and worked his way up, until all the dirt on the steps had simply been shifted down to the step below. Only the top step was clean!

Jacques-Henri, Paul, Bruno and I stood behind him and watched with amazement. David, in a world of his own, had no idea we were there.

'What's he doing?' whispered Bruno.

'Anyone's guess!' said Jacques-Henri.

When David had finished shifting the dirt down the steps, he moved on to the gallery landing and began to sweep dust backwards onto the steps, continuing on his way like an automaton.

'It's best to let him get on with it,' said Jacques-Henri.

And we did. Bruno brushed the steps properly later.

David hadn't been at the Auberge for a week when he decided to leave, unable to cope. Unfortunately, even his return journey went wrong. This was his grand finale. He made it as far as Toulouse, then phoned to say he didn't have enough money with him to buy a train ticket home.

Jacques-Henri had to drive all the way to Toulouse to lend him some. When he got back, about three hours later, he was more relieved David had gone than angry about the trouble he'd caused. Jacques-Henri just raised his arms, as if to say *well, that was a right one there*!

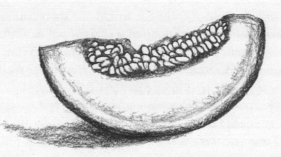

# HERE COME THE
# VASCONES!

I HAD COME TO GASCONY KNOWING A LITTLE ABOUT THE ANCIENT province, and here I was in the deepest countryside learning about it from the inside. To appreciate what makes Gascony so distinctive and separates it from the rest of France, I had to piece together some of its long and fragmented history, which needs to be understood in order to see the land in its true light.

Jacques-Henri showed me an old map of *La Gascogne*. It is bounded by three natural borders. To the north is the sweeping arc of the mighty river Garonne, which follows the shape of a protecting arm, cradling the land in its embrace. To the south are the valleys of the high, forbidding Pyrenees, where Gascony borders the French Basque Country. To the west is the Atlantic coast, the silver shore, from the Bassin d'Arcachon to the mouth of the river Adour. The sea we know in English as the Bay of Biscay is called in French *le Golfe de Gascogne*.

The man-made borders of Gascony have moved backwards and forwards over the natural frontiers. Bordeaux and its vineyards were part of Gascony in the Middle Ages, but are no longer thought of as such. The Béarn, in the central Pyrenees, although associated with Gascony, has a long independent history. Toulouse belongs to the Languedoc, yet is the gateway to Gascony from the east. There is no capital city of Gascony, as the

48

major historical towns – Bordeaux, Bayonne, Toulouse – are all on its frontiers and look to the outside. Gascony is composed of a patchwork of old counties, with strange, hard-to-pronounce names. In the north the Agenais and the Condomois. In the centre Armagnac, Astarac and Fézensaguet. In the west Albret, Chalosse and the Landes. In the south Bigorre, the Couserans and – Jacques-Henri proudly pointed out, the area where we were – the Comminges. Some of these old names cannot be found on modern maps. The administrative *départements* of modern France bear no correlation to the historic Duchy of Gascony.

When I look at a map I see the landscape it represents spreading out as I view it from above. And when I look at a landscape I see the map around me, describing the limits of my view. The old map of Gascony gave me a bird's-eye view to carry in my mind. I was creating my own map.

The landscape varies from the flat, sandy pine forests of the Landes, facing the ocean, through rolling countryside to the foothills of the Pyrenees in the south. In the early part of the year Atlantic breezes reach far inland, bringing nourishing rain. The land is green in spring and dries golden brown in summer, although wetter, greener summers are not unknown. The rivers in the valleys are fed steadily throughout the year with water from the mountains. The small rivers that flow from the high chain of the Pyrenees to become the tributaries of the Garonne form a broad fantail of long ridges and valleys, steeply carved upstream, ever wider and flatter as they approach the plain. Most of the land in Gascony is in some way influenced by the mountains.

Gascony has been inhabited since time immemorial. Early in the twentieth century, in a cave near the village of Lespugue just to the south of Boulogne-sur-Gesse, the oldest piece of sculpture found anywhere in the world was discovered, a small female figurine, thirty thousand years old. The Venus of Lespugue, as she became known, did not remain in Gascony; she was taken to the Musée de l'Homme in Paris. One of the oldest known roads in Europe, the Salt Road, linking the Atlantic with the Mediterranean since the Stone Age, crossed southern Gascony, through Salies-de-Béarn, Pau, Lourdes and Saint-Bertrand-de-Comminges.

Prehistoric Gascony presents an obscure picture of tribes who lived cut off in the mountains, of people who settled the lower land for a while then moved on or were pushed out by incoming tribes, who spoke unknown languages and who didn't record their history, leaving behind only cave paintings, simple artefacts and stone monuments that give little away.

Gascony entered recorded history in 56 BC, during the Roman conquest of Gaul. As the legions marched westwards they crossed the river Garonne at Toulouse, where they came up against people they had never before encountered. The Romans called this new land Aquitaine. Julius Caesar, at the opening of his famous account of the conquest of Gaul, *De Bello Gallico*, clearly stated that the river Garonne marked a frontier: *Gallos ab Aquitanis Garumna flumen... dividit*. Gaul from Aquitaine the river Garonne divides. He wrote that the Aquitanians had a distinct identity, with their own language, laws and way of life. The name Aquitanian is a vague term, referring to the group of thirty or so tribes who inhabited the lands to the west of the Garonne.

While Caesar was engaged in subduing the northern parts of Gaul, he charged General Crassus with conquering Aquitaine. The Aquitanians built a fortified camp on the plain of the river Adour. Their numbers swelled daily with reinforcements from the south, and they attempted to cut off the Roman supply routes. Crassus wasted no time in attacking the camp. The Aquitanians resisted fiercely, hurling stones and javelins from their ramparts at the attacking Romans, but they had left the rear entrance to the camp unsecured. A cohort of Roman soldiers made their way inside, unnoticed, while the battle was raging at the other end. The Aquitanians, finding themselves trapped, broke out of the camp in panic and began to run across the plain. The Roman cavalry pursued them, slaughtering them as they fled. As news of the massacre spread, other Aquitanian tribes submitted to the Romans; all but the most remote tribes inhabiting the Pyrenees, who relied on the onset of winter and the mountains to save them.

The Aquitanians gradually became Romanised, adopting Latin as their language, absorbing the Roman religion and customs. Under the *pax Romana*, Aquitaine became a prosperous province of the Empire. Good roads were built linking the main towns, trade flourished and the locals felt safe to move out of their fortified villages and settle on the fertile land in the valleys. The Romans of course enjoyed the baths created over the thermal springs rising where the high valleys met the plain.

The Barbarian invasions began in AD 407, bringing in a period of instability, when populations across Europe were on the move. The Visigoths made Gascony part of their kingdom, until they were pushed out by the Franks – the Germanic tribe who would later give their name to the land they settled, France. Meanwhile, on the other side of the Pyrenees, the Vascones were waiting. They were a tough, stubborn lot, living high in the Cantabrian mountains around the headwaters of the river Ebro. Protected by their position, they had escaped the influence of Roman rule, preserving their ancient tribal language and traditions. In the late sixth century the Vascones began to migrate across the Pyrenees. At first they made brief raids, taking advantage of the anarchy that prevailed in the lowlands. Soon they began to migrate in substantial numbers. The reasons for this move are unclear: it could have been the pressure of population, the desire to leave the mountains and move down to more productive land, or the conflict that seems to have begun about that time with their neighbours to the east. When the Vascones first moved down from the mountains, they were a marauding band of cut-throats, destroying crops, ripping up vines and setting fire to sheep pens, but before long they had settled and made good. As the Vascones made the land their home, they gave it their name, Vasconia, which later took the form Gascony.

In the year 602, the Frankish kings appointed a Duke of Gascony in an attempt at controlling the unruly Gascons, but it didn't work. The Gascons were a law unto themselves and they fought the French armies using the natural fortifications of the mountains and the forests, where they could hide, ambush and disappear. In a similar way as the cartoon character Astérix the Gaul, in his village by the sea, refused to submit to the Romans, so the Gascons in their isolated land resisted the power of the faraway French kings. The Gascon historian Louis Barrau-Dihigo wrote that Gascony was too far from the political centres of the kingdom for the authority of the kings of France to be felt in any effective way. It was inevitable that an independent state would form between the Pyrenees, the ocean and the Garonne, and this is just what happened.

The Gascons had a habit of assassinating the envoys sent to rule over them by the French. Their natural affinities lay to the south, with the kingdoms of Navarre and Aragon. The Gascon chiefs went across the Pyrenees to find a leader. In 864, Sans-Mittara, the youngest son of the Prince of Navarre, was elected Duke of Gascony. The name Sans in Gascon is the equivalent of Sancho in Spanish. The epithet Mittara meant 'the terrible'. So Sancho-the-Terrible, a character shrouded in mystery, was the first of the hereditary Dukes of Gascony. His son and the next Duke of Gascony was Garcia-Sans, followed by Sans-Garcia. Confused? You will be! The next Duke was Sans-Sans, followed by Guilhem-Sans, Bernat-Guilhem and Sans-Guilhem. Well, why waste a good name or two?

The Dukes of Gascony were a legendary dynasty, yet little is known of them apart from their names. These were feudal times. Gascony was a land of fiefdoms, where each local count had a mind of his own and there were many local conflicts. Perhaps it reveals something about the Gascon temperament that when left to their own devices, they were too busy getting on with living or fighting one another to bother writing things down.

# GASCONNADE

THE LONG AND DISTINCTIVE HISTORY OF GASCONY, AND THE qualities of the land, have left their imprint on the people. The Gascon character is unique and complex, difficult to define, steeped in local traditions and for outsiders rich in stereotypes.

The French outside Gascony think the Gascons are boastful. The word *gasconnade* means telling unlikely stories, bragging about one's own abilities, exaggerating one's achievements. Rodomontade. Fanfaronade. *Gasconnade*. Jean de La Fontaine, in his *Fables*, wrote about a Gascon who couldn't stop boasting, who went from *gasconnade* to *gasconnade*, until his friends brought him down to size. Jean Froissart, in his famous *Chronicles* of the fourteenth century, was also unkind about the Gascons, describing them as unstable, greedy and opportunistic. In his view Gascons were fickle and inclined to follow – or rebel against – the master of the moment, as it suited them.

Gascons had to use their wits and seize the moment in order to survive. Throughout the centuries the Gascon land, although pleasant, has never been easy to cultivate. In many ways life on the land has always been tough. The Gascon farmer is often at the mercy of the elements, whether he is a shepherd on the high mountain pastures, a cowherd in the foothills, a vine grower on the lower hills or an arable farmer down on the plain. Sometimes the soil can be unyielding, the spring rains too heavy or the summer sun too fierce. Farmers have to be adaptable and resourceful, and they have to understand their environment. Making the land productive takes knowledge and skill. Working the land gave the Gascons a reputation for being hardy and brave. There is an old saying: *Si le terrain est ingrat, semez-y des Gascons, ils pousseront partout*! If the soil is unyielding, plant some Gascons in it, they'll grow anywhere. The Gascons are often thought of as being hospitable and charitable, as if the difficult life on the land has taught them the value of extending kindness to others.

Hard times led many to become adventurers and fortune seekers. They were good soldiers; renowned for their courage in battle, they often hired themselves out as mercenaries. Some Gascons made dashing military figures. Gascony's most famous son was the legendary Charles de Batz-Castelmore, better known as D'Artagnan, the swashbuckling musketeer. His character showed the proverbial Gascon traits of swaggering hot-headedness, tenacity and courage to the point of reckless bravado, all combined in an oh-so-likeable persona, eternally 20 years old. Like a good Gascon, D'Artagnan left his life shrouded in mystery and legend, for others to write stories about. He spent most of his time away from Gascony in the service of his kings. He was at the famous siege of Arras in Flanders, he fought for Charles I of England at the battle of Newbury, he was charged with arresting the infamous embezzling finance minister Fouquet at Nantes in Brittany, he was appointed Governor of Lille, and on a glorious June day in 1673 he was shot down, a hero, at the siege of Maastricht in the Netherlands. Always he led from the front, swelled with Gascon pride, distinguished as much by his - colourful language and earthy accent as by his bravery.

You can take the man out of Gascony, but you can't take Gascony out of the man!

When Edmond Rostand wrote his play *Cyrano de Bergerac* at the end of the nineteenth century, he made his hero a typical Gascon, a mixture of the real-life Cyrano de Bergerac and the popular myths surrounding D'Artagnan, with a dash of the Garonne in his veins and a flicker of the Pyrenees in his eyes. The real Cyrano de Bergerac of the seventeenth century was a free-thinker, a braggart, a soldier, a duallist, a lover, grotesque in his appearance, famed for his enormous nose; he was also an original writer of burlesque stories and eccentric science fiction. Rostand's Cyrano is the leader of a band of cadets, all of them proud, mad, gallant Gascons, who boast about being Gascon, sing about being Gascon – *Ce sont les cadets de Gascogne* – listen to the music of a shepherd's flute to remind them of Gascony, are quick to draw their sword, fond of the all-important gesture, and get drunk on the smell of gunpowder in battle. United by honour, the cadets look out for each other and are delighted when their haughty regimental commander, the Comte de Guiche, lets his proper French accent slip and reveals himself to be a Gascon, one of their own after all! Cyrano, to compensate for his nose, has a poet's soul and a way with words, and if he fails to win fair lady, it's because his boastfulness hides a deep-seated modesty and he puts friendship before love.

Rostand's Cyrano is a nostalgic creation, a dream of how old Gascony should have been. Let's not forget, the real Savinien Cyrano de Bergerac was not a Gascon at all, he was a Parisian; his name Bergerac does not come from the town of that name on the river Dordogne, it was the name of an estate in the Chevreuse valley near Paris. No one knows for sure if he really had such a big nose.

If D'Artagnan and Cyrano showed how the fiery Gascon temperament could turn out well, the feudal Counts of Armagnac demonstrated how it could go horribly wrong. They had caused trouble for generations: they refused to submit to the wishes of any king and regularly started feuds with their neighbours. Their unruliness reached its peak in Count Jean V of Armagnac. Unusual in appearance, he was a short, chubby man, with his neck set into his shoulders, a pock-marked face, long red hair, and eyes that looked in different directions. He was bad tempered and lacked the energy to see any project through to its conclusion. He did exactly what he wanted

Count Jean had a long relationship with his beautiful younger sister Isabelle. He called her affectionately *ma mia costa*, my own rib, an allusion to the story of Adam and Eve. Brother and sister had three children, the Bastards of Armagnac, two boys and a girl, whom Isabelle referred to discreetly as her niece and nephews; which in a sense they were. The Count asked the Pope for special dispensation to marry Isabelle. The Pope refused, so Jean forged a papal Bull to celebrate their marriage. When the Pope found out, he was furious and excommunicated the incestuous Count. Eventually Jean had to settle for marrying a woman to whom he was not related.

Count Jean antagonised the Kings of France even more than he upset the Pope. He openly rebelled against King Charles VII, behaving like a local king himself. When the Dauphin was in dispute with his father, Jean sided with the insubordinate heir to the throne. The king sent an army to crush the rebellious vassal, confiscated his property and forced him into exile in Catalonia. The following year, when the Dauphin succeeded his father as King Louis XI, he allowed the Count of Armagnac to return home and restored his property. Having returned home, the count turned against his former ally.

After years of trouble, the French had had enough of the Armagnacs and sent another army to sort out the intractable rebel once and for all. When the end finally came in 1473, Count Jean had brought it on himself. He made a last stand against the French from his stronghold in the walled town of Lectoure, on a lofty promontory high above the plain of the Gers. The French laid siege to the town and, after a couple of hard winter months, the king offered to make a deal: the count's previous misdeeds would be forgiven, an amnesty would be granted for him and his family, the town would be spared, and in return he would recognise the will of the king. The count accepted the deal and on 4 March peace was declared.

Two days later the town gates were opened and the French army entered with their ensigns flying. An apparently accidental scuffle broke out – no doubt premeditated – and the French turned on the count and the townspeople. One French soldier stabbed Count Jean through the heart while another smashed his skull with an axe. They weren't taking any chances. His body was dragged through the streets for the soldiers to hack as it went by. The French went on the rampage, slaughtered most of the menfolk, sacked and burned the town and demolished the ramparts. The long-suffering countess, who was seven months pregnant with the couple's first child, was taken to the Château de Buzet and locked in a cell with what was left of her husband's body. Perhaps not surprisingly, her child was stillborn a month later. It was rumoured that the French guards gave her a potion to induce a miscarriage, to ensure the extinction of the House of Armagnac. These were gruesome times. What we would call war crimes nowadays were merely sideshows in the Middle Ages.

The County of Armagnac subsequently became a royal domain and the town of Lectoure was gradually rebuilt. When I visited I stayed at the Hôtel de Bastard, an elegant eighteenth-century mansion near the old ramparts; despite its name, the present owners are welcoming hosts and quite charming. For breakfast they serve excellent *rillettes d'oie*, shredded goose – very Gascon, but a goose too far for some! The town has a forlorn, aristocratic air, as if at heart it has never truly recovered from that treacherous assault in the early spring of 1473.

Whatever others might say about them, the Gascons are a proud breed. In the words of the Gascon social historian Pierre Veilletet: *Soyez Gascons, que diable! On n'est jamais assez Gascon*. Be Gascon, damn it. You can never be too Gascon.

In Jacques-Henri Cazagnac I'd found the friendly face of Gascony, a descendant of those stubborn, unruly, fun-loving Gascons of old. He lived up to the image of the honest, jovial Gascon, who shouldn't be taken seriously all the time. Whether he was welcoming guests to the Auberge or teaching me how things worked at the farm, he had a sense of being the principal actor on his stage. No more trouble making, of course: Jacques-Henri just wanted to have a nice time, tipple away at his Armagnac and look after his family. He had faith in his own values and he trusted the people he knew best. He didn't trust banks, he wasn't sure what they might do with his money.

I heard a rumour that he had a pot of money buried some-where under the floor of the barn, although I never saw any evidence of it.

# ENGLAND'S VINEYARD

'Y OU ARE A GODON,' JACQUES-HENRI SAID TO ME.
'Pardon?'

*Godon* is an old Gascon name for an Englishman, from the time when the Gascons fought alongside English soldiers during the Hundred Years War, because of the English soldiers' habit of swearing 'Goddam'. Well, I thought, it was better than being a *Rosbif*.

I was beginning to feel at home in Gascony, and with good reason. A special relationship once existed between England and Gascony. The shifting alliances of mediaeval Europe brought the two together by a combination of chance and one strong-willed woman.

In the eleventh century Gascony had become part of the Duchy of Aquitaine, whose territory extended over nearly all of southwest France south of the Loire. The lands of the kings of France covered a small area of northern central France. Although Aquitaine paid homage to the kings of France, the dukes of Aquitaine were wealthier than the French kings and Aquitaine was effectively independent. In 1137, Duke William X of Aquitaine succeeded in marrying off his beautiful red-haired daughter and sole heir, Eleanor, to King Louis VII of France. Eleanor of Aquitaine was the richest heiress in Christendom; uniting Aquitaine and France seemed like a coup for both sides. Eleanor and Louis were married for fifteen years and they had two daughters, but the marriage was not to last. Eleanor was lively and spirited, Louis cold and monkish, so they were hopelessly incompatible, and in March 1152 the marriage was annulled, on the grounds that they were cousins and should never have been married in the first place.

Eleanor retained all the lands she had inherited from her father, about a quarter of present-day France – probably the biggest divorce settlement in history! Less than two months after the annulment of her marriage, this *femme formidable* married the ambitious and charismatic young Henry Plantagenet. The wedding took place in a secret ceremony in May 1152. Eleanor was 30, Henry just 19. At the time he was Duke of Normandy and Count of Anjou.

Eleanor's second marriage changed the course of history. Two years later, in 1154, Henry succeeded to the throne of England as King Henry II, with Eleanor as his queen. Gascony became the southernmost land of the great Plantagenet empire, stretching from Berwick-upon-Tweed to the Pyrenees. So began the long association between England and Gascony that was to endure for the next three hundred years, give or take a year or so.

English officials were sent out to administer the province of Gascony. The governor was known as the *Lieutenant du Roi*, a viceroy appointed by the king of England to represent his interests. Gascon nobles visited England often to gain knowledge of English ways and administrative methods, before returning to take up positions back home. Anglo-Gascon coins were struck in various towns in Gascony. Gascon military nobles, ever ready for adventure, fought alongside Englishmen against the French, the Welsh and the Scots. Some were rewarded for their efforts with grants of land in England.

Considering the distance and the cost of the journey, the extent of the comings and goings was astonishing for the age.

English and Gascon men and women settled and made new lives for themselves in one another's countries. Many English merchants became citizens of Bordeaux, Saintes, Agen and Toulouse. The town of Libourne on the river Dordogne took its name from Sir Roger de Leyburn, *Lieutenant du Roi*, who established the port there in 1270. The small town of Bâa, founded in 1287 near Bordeaux, got its name because the land there belonged to the Bishop of Bath and Wells and the locals couldn't pronounce Bath. The area known as Guienne, to the southeast of Bordeaux, was so called because the English couldn't pronounce Aquitaine. The small town of Hastingues, up river from the port of Bayonne, was named after – no surprise – Hastings.

Gascony was a prosperous province for England. The relationship was characterised by one aspect above all: commerce. And this commerce was defined by one product: wine. From the beginning of the thirteenth century the English encouraged wine production in Gascony and provided the almost exclusive market for its export. When a mediaeval Englishman talked of wine, he had in mind only the wine of Gascony. The development of the vineyards by the English was a boon for the province: its soils and climate were well suited to the vine, and large areas of quite barren land were improved and made fertile for vines to be cultivated commercially. The maps that still designate many of the vineyards of the Bordelais were drawn at this time, such as those forming the jurisdiction of Saint-Emilion, fixed by Edward I in 1289. The English formed the *Jurade* to administer the town of Saint-Emilion and make sure the wine flowed freely. In the cavernous underground church carved out of the rock beneath the town, traces of painted English roses can still be seen decorating the ceiling, reminders of the English love of Gascon wine and the affection the Gascons had for the English who bought their wine.

Bordeaux was the thriving commercial centre of the Anglo-Gascon wine trade. Its position at the confluence of the Garonne and the Dordogne, at the head of the estuary of the Gironde, made it a natural trading port. Bordeaux had old links with the British Isles. As far back as the first century BC, records tell of an ancient British wine merchant set up in business on the waterfront at Bordeaux. In the Middle Ages, the trade with England brought about a massive and sustained economic boom; the city doubled in size during the first half of the thirteenth century. Great fairs took place when the ships arrived from England to collect the new vintage. English traders and mariners congregated in the Rocela district of the city, near the quays where their ships moored. The Rocela district is now the Rue de la Rousselle. With a population of around 30,000, not much less than London at the time, Bordeaux was in a sense England's second city. The names of its mayors tell their own story: Sandwich, Swynburne, Molton, Lutherell, Bukton, Radcliff, Merbury and Redford. King Louis XI later acknowledged that if Bordeaux was one of the greatest and most populous cities in his kingdom, it owed its wealth to the English, who brought gold and silver that they converted into Gascon wine.

The demand for wine was considerable and Gascony exported enormous quantities to slake the thirsts of mediaeval Englishmen and women. The English liked the light, young red wines produced around Bordeaux, at Pessac, Barsac, Saint-Macaire, Langon and Saint-Emilion. This clear new wine was known in French as *clairet*; the English acquired a taste for it and called it claret. What would mediaeval claret have tasted like? We can only speculate. It would certainly have been younger than modern Bordeaux red and would probably have been much lighter, with the refreshing cut of a present-day Beaujolais nouveau. The idea of vintage wine did not exist, as wine would barely keep until the next year's harvest and usually from late spring it was unpalatable. Glass bottles were not yet used; wine was stored and transported in 240-gallon wooden barrels known as *tonneaux*.

The great mediaeval wine fleets left Bordeaux *en masse* each autumn, laden with the new vintage and bound for English ports: Plymouth, Bristol, Southampton, Winchelsea, Sandwich, London, Boston and Hull. Wines from the south of Gascony were exported through the port of Bayonne, on the river Adour. The wine ships were called cogs, their rounded, capacious hulls carrying 200 *tonneaux* per vessel; although the biggest cogs, the super-tankers of their day, carried 300 *tonneaux*. According to the records, in the year 1300 no fewer than 900 cogs left Bordeaux for England. The crossing to London could be made in about ten to twelve days, but delays and stopovers for victuals meant it often took longer. The constant plying back and forth of the wine ships greatly improved the seafaring skills of the English merchant navy. 1309 was *the* bumper year for the wine trade, with over twenty-five million gallons imported. That's over six gallons of Gascon wine for the year for every man, woman and child in England.

Many Gascon wine merchants set up businesses in London, for which they were given economic incentives in the form of trading privileges and reduced duties. Some commercial districts of London became 'Gasconised'. An area near the Vintry wharves on the Thames was known as La Riole, because it was frequented by so many merchants from the town of La Réole on the Garonne. The Gascon merchants in London established their own professional association, the Merchant Wine Tonners of Gascoyne, based around the church of St Martin in the Vintry. One wine merchant left his native Bergerac to set up in London and eventually rose to become the King's Chamberlain and Taker of Wines. Wine in mediaeval times was subject to all sorts of regulations and duties and was taxed several times en route. *Plus ça change*!

In exchange for wine, England supplied Gascony with corn, wool, cloth and dried and salted fish, especially herring, hake and salmon. England even exported preserved meat and cheese to Gascony. These exports made the outward journey profitable for the merchant venturers who had to lay out huge sums of money to finance the voyages. England and Gascony needed each other. When England was at war and limits were imposed on the export of corn, an exception was usually made for Gascony. In return, more wine was bought to keep the troops happy.

Wine jugs were imported from Gascony. These were luxury items for well-to-do English families and were more finely crafted than the jugs made in England. They were hard earthenware, usually with floral designs in yellow, green and brown, finished with a thin salt glaze. A feature was the spout, pinched with the thumb into the shape of a beak. A continuous rim behind this spout stopped any sediment and allowed the wine to pour freely without spillage. There is a good example in Carisbrooke Castle on the Isle of Wight.

Gascony supplied England with that other essential commodity for mediaeval living: salt. It was obtained from the evaporation of seawater in the lagoons along the western shore. The action of the tides, the warm winds blowing off the ocean and the hot southern sun on the bays and inlets along the flat coastline made ideal conditions for salt extraction. As the seawater reduced in the salt pans, the salt would crystallise in the shallower parts. Barefoot salt panners, wearing broad caps to protect themselves from the relentless glare of the sun, used long-handled wooden shovels to push the salt into heaps, which they covered with straw and then left to dry in the open. Once dry, the salt was shovelled into sacks. The trade was highly lucrative – in the Middle Ages salt was known as 'white gold'. It was a valuable resource in an age when it was almost the only means of preserving food.

The Gascon language flourished under English rule. Eleanor of Aquitaine and Henry Plantagenet's most famous son, Richard Coeur de Lion, wrote poetry in Gascon. This was the age of the Troubadours, the minstrel-poets from across the pleasure-loving provinces of southern France, who composed love songs about gallant knights and fair ladies. Troubadours were often accompanied by *jongleurs*, all-round entertainers with a variety of tricks in their routine. The Gascons were renowned *jongleurs*, performing popular songs along with juggling and acrobatic stunts. They were especially admired for their military dart-throwing skills.

Péguilhan almost has a famous son in the Troubadour Aimeric de Péguilhan; I say almost because he was born at Toulouse, around 1175, the son of a cloth merchant. He probably had a family connection with Péguilhan. Aimeric was a wandering minstrel, ending his days in Lombardy in 1230. According to his contemporaries, he was a good songwriter but a bad singer.

Times weren't always peaceful, but on the whole the three centuries of English rule in Gascony were a time of growth and good fortune. The English made Gascony a colony in the true sense of the word, from *colonia*, meaning a farm. The negative impact of English rule in Gascony was that so much land was planted with vines that Gascony could not grow enough food to feed itself and became dependent on imports from England, but on balance this was profitable for the growers and the merchants on both sides.

England's empire in Europe shrank through the course of the fourteenth and fifteenth centuries. Only Gascony remained an English-ruled enclave in the southwest. The endless hostilities between England and France during the Hundred Years War cut off the land route, leaving Gascony reachable only by sea. The sea passage could be perilous; with limited navigation equipment, the ships had to hug the coast and were vulnerable to pirates and bad weather.

The English tired of their colony: it was far away, and difficult and expensive to maintain. The French were no longer prepared to tolerate the presence of the *Godons* in what they regarded as their land. The French army fought its way ruthlessly through Gascony, taking it piece by piece, as Anglo-Gascon resistance gradually crumbled. King Charles VII, after years of war and wrangling, succeeded in wresting the province away from English control. The decisive battle took place at Castillon-la-Bataille, on the river Dordogne, in July 1453. Lord Talbot, the commander of the Anglo-Gascon army, was impetuous and, believing false rumours of a French retreat, attacked with only part of his forces. Some said he charged without his lance or his sword. The battle turned into a rout. Many Anglo-Gascon soldiers drowned in the river as they fled and Talbot was slain. Castillon has been described as the Waterloo of Gascon nationality.

Bordeaux was the last city to fall to the French. It had always been the most loyal bastion of English rule in Gascony. The Bordelais did not want to become French, nor did they want to lose their lucrative trade with England. The French army laid siege to the city from August to October of 1453. The Bordelais, supported by the English garrison in the city, held out through the siege for as long as they could. When the city finally surrendered, the English who were left there were escorted to the coast under safe conduct, by heralds and men-at-arms, to return to England by sea. The Bordelais city governors and many local leaders left with them; refusing allegiance to the French crown, they abandoned their native land to take refuge in England. On 19 October the banners of France were unfurled over the city walls, signalling the end of English Gascony. The French, to be fair, allowed the English another six months to ship out the 1453 wine vintage – after all, trade had to go on and the growers and merchants had to stay in business.

The fall of Bordeaux brought about the demise of the Anglo-Gascon wine trade. The vineyards of Gascony became so depleted that only after the Second World War did wine production in Gascony again reach the levels it had achieved during the prosperous years of the early 1300s. The vineyards around Bordeaux and along the Médoc peninsula benefited from substantial investments by aristocrats during the eighteenth century and bankers and entrepreneurs during the nineteenth century, but in Gascony as a whole, wine production took five hundred years to recover from the departure of the English.

Whereas the English had allowed the Gascons to speak Gascon and to retain their Gascon identity, the French made them speak French and tried to make French subjects out of them. The Gascon tongue nevertheless remained the popular language among country people and the language of folklore.

Having conquered Gascony, the French made little investment in it. Over the centuries that followed it became a forgotten backwater. The isolation in the countryside and the stubborn, steadfast character of the people meant that Gascony kept its own traditions and its sense of independence. Paris was seen as another country. A Gascon heading there would be said to be 'going to France'.

The Anglo-Gascon legacy in the southwest caused English ways of thinking to leave their mark on French literature. Two of France's greatest writers – Montaigne and Montesquieu, who also happened to be Gascons – kept the spirit of independence alive. The humanist writer Michel de Montaigne, famous for his essays, whose château lay to the east of Bordeaux, close to Castillon-la-Bataille, thought himself more a Gascon than a Frenchman. His great-grandfather had been a Bordeaux merchant, trading in wine, salt fish and woad. He patriotically referred to the defeated English commander Lord Talbot as 'our' Talbot. In a letter to a friend dated 1570, Montaigne complained that he was having difficulty getting his work published 'up there' in Paris, where they considered his Gascon style unpolished.

The family seat of the Enlightenment *philosophe* Charles de Secondat, Baron de Montesquieu, was the Château de La Brède, a turreted fortress standing in an idyllic setting, on a lake of running water, fed by a natural spring rising beneath the château, a few kilometres to the south of Bordeaux. Montesquieu loved his family home and spent every summer there until the grapes had been harvested in his vineyards. Montesquieu's mother tongue was Gascon: he spoke Gascon with the locals, *les gens du coin*, and French with his fellow aristocrats and literary friends. Montesquieu travelled in England and was impressed by the English system of government, which he wanted to see adopted in *ancien régime* France. He was pragmatic and forward thinking – traits the French begrudgingly attribute to the English. In the 1730s, the French authorities introduced restrictions on the planting of new vineyards, and Montesquieu saw this as protectionism by the established producers. He knew many of the wine merchants who traded in Bordeaux and he vociferously opposed the ban. What did they want to do, give the new business to the Portuguese?

The old alliance between England and Gascony has been forgotten. But it is tempting to speculate: even after five and a half centuries of being officially part of France, do some affinities remain between England and Gascony? Where do the Gascons get their simple and dry sense of humour? Why is rugby their favourite sport? How did they make the classic English culinary association between duck and green peas? Until recently, two of the most popular makes of car bought in Gascony were Rovers and Land Rovers. Even today, driving along the esplanades in the coastal resorts of Arcachon and Cap Ferret, typical status symbols for the wealthy are Range Rovers and Aston Martins. And the Gascons seem to feel closer in some ways to England than they do to northern France. Jacques-Henri once remarked pithily: 'Everything north of the Loire is not France!'

# BREAKDOWN BEND

THE KITCHEN GARDEN, THE CASAU, OCCUPIED THE AREA JUST behind the farmhouse. Its sole purpose was to supply the vegetable needs of the family and the restaurant. Local speciality vegetables were grown to give the menu an authentic flavour. The main crops were haricots, courgettes, *cornichons*, peas, artichokes, potatoes, lettuce, onions and garlic.

Two spreading rosemary bushes stood sentinel, one on each side of the main path into the *casau*. It became a quiet ritual for me, each time I entered the garden, to run my hand through the fragrant foliage or pinch off a hard, narrow leaf to smell. I find the scent of rosemary delicious in small doses, but sickening if inhaled too deeply. Other aromatic herbs were planted among the vegetables: parsley, sage, marjoram, tarragon, fennel and thyme. Taking pride of place in the middle of the plot was a bay tree, known in French as a *laurier-noble* or a *laurier-sauce*, depending on whether it is viewed as a fine tree or a culinary ingredient.

There was no hosepipe for watering the vegetables as there was for the tomatoes; the whole garden was watered laboriously by hand, using an old galvanised watering can kept tucked behind one of the rosemary bushes and filled from a cobalt blue plastic water butt standing by the top wall. The wooden handle of the watering can was worn hard and smooth from years of use. It was heavy to carry and awkward to hold. In addition to frequent watering, the *casau* needed constant work, some of it hard, such as hoeing the weeds, digging the onions and furrowing the potatoes.

Paul and I were picking the daily list of vegetables for Marie-Jeanne. We picked the onions first. Paul brandished a two-pronged fork with a short wooden handle, called a *binette*. He set to work along the row, loosening the soil with the fork, while I collected the onions in a wooden tray.

'Do you see the yellow colour of the onions?' he asked me. 'They're called *jaune paille*.' Straw yellow.

We moved on to the garlic. This time it was my turn to swing the fork and Paul's turn to pick up the garlic.

'This type of pink garlic is called *violet de Cadours*,' Paul told me. *'C'est typique de la région.'* He broke open a bulb to show me.

Having finished with the alliums, we picked a couple of lettuces and a handful of herbs. Finally, it was Paul's turn again with the *binette*, working his way along the ridge while I gathered handfuls of small new potatoes and put them in another wooden tray.

We put the trays in the back of the van, clambered through the passenger door into the front and set off for the Auberge. Paul flung the 2CV over the crest of the hill and down into the dip. The engine made a spluttering noise, then died.

*'Aïeeeeeee!* What's happening?' he exclaimed, almost loosing control of the vehicle. It slewed from side to side with no power.

The van slowed down as it went up the slope on the other side of the dip. We veered to the left and coasted onto the grass verge. The old crate bumped over the uneven ground, until we came to a stop on the bank. We looked at each other, surprised.

'What happened?' I asked.

'*Sais pas*,' said Paul. Dunno.

We got out and looked under the bonnet, but we couldn't see anything wrong. There was nothing we could do. We decided to sit on the bank and wait until someone passed who would give us a lift the rest of the way back to Péguilhan.

Paul asked if I wanted a cigarette. Sure. He fetched his packet of Drum tobacco and OCB papers from the van, and we each rolled a cigarette and smoked, contemplatively, in the sunshine.

'This reminds me of my *service militaire*,' said Paul.

'Why's that?' I asked, not seeing the connection.

'Sitting around, doing nothing, killing time,' he told me. Paul had completed his compulsory ten-month military service only a few weeks earlier.

'We had to stand around on sentry duty for hours, marking time until the end of the watch. Or else we had to do some pointless task, like polishing our boots, or unpacking and repacking our kit, or painting things white, over and over again. It was stupid. A complete waste of time.'

'So the army wasn't for you, then?' I asked.

'You must be joking!' Paul replied. 'And I didn't even get to see the world, most of the time I was stationed just down the road in the barracks at Tarbes.'

'Do you know what you want to *do* in life?' I asked.

'No, I don't. I would like to see more of the world, I've always lived here in Péguilhan, but I think it's inevitable that I'll take over the farm one day. Imagine if I told my father that I didn't want to go into farming. He'd be so disappointed.'

Paul shrugged his shoulders. 'What about you, do you know what you want to do?' he asked me.

'No idea either.'

We stubbed out our cigarette ends in the soil, carefully, making sure not to set fire to the dry grass.

'We've been waiting here for ages, haven't we?' I said. 'Not one car has come by. Do you think we should walk?'

'Perhaps that's not a bad idea,' agreed Paul.

Just when we were on the point of setting off on foot for Péguilhan, Jacques-Henri drew up in the Renault. He stopped the car, leant out of the window, laughed at us and asked what was up. '*Alors quoi*, what are you doing there?'

'The 2CV broke down.'

'And you're just sitting there?'

'What else could we do?'

He thought we looked *ridicule*. 'Marie-Jeanne wants to know where the vegetables are.'

Jacques-Henri soon discovered that the 2CV had run out of petrol. We insisted it wasn't our fault, the fuel gauge was broken, but he wasn't impressed.

# DOGS AND SHEEP

I WAS DAUNTED AT FIRST BY THE RESPONSIBILITY OF GUARDING the flock of sheep. I could only guess at what might be involved. Being a shepherd had romantic connotations for me, but these were soon dispelled.

Jacques-Henri took me through the drill. The sheep were put into their barn, *la bergerie*, every night to keep them safe from the wolves that roamed the woods. They were let out in the morning to graze in the open pasture, brought back to the *bergerie* in the middle of the day to protect them from the heat, and taken out again for a few hours in the afternoon.

In the morning, the sheep were packed tightly in the *bergerie*. A warm fug filled the air. *Pfwah!* The barn's wood-clad inner walls were treacle-brown, the colour of years of sheep fug. The animals stood docilely, waiting to be let out. We opened the gate and they started spilling out into the farmyard, jumping over each other in excitement, bleating with joy, their heads bobbing up and down. The two sheepdogs ran around with an excess of energy. If a sheep left the flock, one of the dogs gave it a nip on the back leg to remind it who was in charge, and it plunged headlong back among the others. Jacques-Henri told me to look out for the lead sheep – *la meneuse* – whom the others would follow. It was easy to spot her at the front of the flock, with her head held high.

We left the farmyard and made our way down the hill towards the open pasture. The sheep formed a living mass that wheeled around and changed shape. When they reached the pasture, they spread out and started grazing. Eating focused their minds and they calmed down.

The flock consisted of about a hundred and fifty ewes, *les brebis*, two active rams, *les béliers*, and two castrated rams, *les moutons*. The sheep were Berrichons, a breed originating in central France, good all-rounders, physically well suited to the pastures around Péguilhan and with an easy temperament. Jacques-Henri assured me that Berrichon sheep produce excellent meat, their gigots – a subject close to his heart – being particularly well developed.

'*Ce Berrichon, il n'est pas maigrichon!*' he said, happily. It's not skinny.

The sheepdogs were named Labrit and Mizou. They had a son called Rôti, meaning roast.

Labrit was the boss. He was named simply after his breed, the typical sheepdog of southwest France. Labrits are small dogs, about the size of a terrier, not at all like the sheepdogs we use in the British Isles. Their coat is rough, brown over the body, grey on the face and down the legs, shaggy, curling at the ends. They have quite long legs for their size and are very agile. Labrit exemplified the qualities of his breed: perky, curious, cheeky and very reliable.

His girlfriend Mizou was smaller, of mixed and indeterminate breed. She had a short, dense, light brown coat, speckled dark brown. She was sturdy but fast.

Rôti was a tiny, wiry, yellow-haired hooligan, with no sense of what being a sheepdog was about. His name seemed fitting: he looked like a small chicken roasted before it had been plucked properly. He would charge into the middle of the flock, sending the sheep off in every direction, then run around in circles yapping for no apparent reason. Labrit and Mizou preferred to keep their distance, clearly embarrassed by their delinquent offspring. Rôti was more of a hindrance than a help, and after his unsuccessful trials at the farm he was moved to the Auberge. There was even talk of finding him a new home. I felt sorry for the reject.

The dogs were bilingual in French and Gascon. Of course, they didn't understand English. Labrit and Mizou were clever and a lot could be conveyed with the intonation of the voice, but I had to learn the proper commands.

### GASCON SHEPHERD'S PHRASEBOOK

| GASCON | FRENCH | ENGLISH |
|--------|--------|---------|
| quèrretz! | allez! | go and get them! |
| tèrra! | couchez! | stay and lie flat! |
| poncha la! | mords-la! | bite it! |
| plasèr | doucement | gently does it |
| aci! | ici! | heel! |

If I didn't give the correct command, Labrit would look at me impatiently.

I had to keep my wits about me. The fields were unfenced. The flock had to be steered away from the edge of the woods, where the stragglers and the independent minded would sometimes disappear. I moved the sheep around different parts of each field and from one field to another, in order to even out the rate at which they ate the grass, as it dried out through the summer. Their favourite food was the lush grass in the bottom of the dry valley to the west of the farm. It was an ongoing job to keep them from wandering wherever they pleased and eating just whatever they wanted.

One of the active rams clearly didn't want me there. He had the most enormous testicles. They hung down between his hind legs like a pair of skittles in a woolly bag, almost reaching the ground. I wondered how he didn't hurt himself as he walked: they swung from side to side, banging against his legs.

A showdown between me and the ram with the giant gonads was inevitable. He thought he had me cornered against a tree. His head was down, as if he was going to butt me. He started moving forward slightly. This didn't look good. He charged, I jumped out of the way and he rammed the tree. Ouch! That had to hurt. Big balls, no brains, it seemed.

I improvised a shepherd's crook from a stick I found in the woods, then chose a tree stump where I could sit and watch the flock. Labrit and Mizou hunkered down in the long grass, keeping an eye on the sheep who grazed happily, creating a gentle background noise of ripping grass. There was harmony in the way they slowly moved across the pasture. Now and again a frisson ran through the flock, then they settled down again. As for Billy Big Balls, he was trying to reassert his potency by mounting a few ewes, who weren't too interested in his attentions.

A shepherd's job was a solitary occupation. Sitting in the sunny meadow, carefree and content, tending the flock with a pair of sheepdogs, I thought to myself – *this was worth coming to Gascony for*!

I remember Jacques-Henri coming to look for me once. I'd been out with the sheep for a couple of hours and he needed me to work at the Auberge. He saw me standing on the tree stump, my crook over my shoulder, my hand shielding my eyes from the sun, as I watched the sheep in the field.

'*Comme Robinson Crusoë sur son île,*' he said, as he approached. Like Robinson Crusoe on his island. Afterwards, I thought about what he'd said: he was right, it was like living on an island.

'Is it really true that sheep are stupid?' I asked Jacques-Henri.

'They can sense things,' he told me, 'in the atmosphere and in the earth, which you and I are not aware of.'

'They act stupid sometimes,' I said.

'They're nervous, not stupid,' he said, bluntly.

Jacques-Henri had respect for his sheep. He firmly believed that animals gave better meat when they had lived free and happy lives *au grand air*, eating naturally, exposed to the elements and the changes of the seasons.

We picked out two sheep at a time to be slaughtered. We chose animals that were a little bigger than lambs, but still not fully grown. Jacques-Henri grabbed at their hind legs to select the good ones. While the flock was in the *bergerie*, we dragged the two chosen sheep into a small side pen. They sensed something was wrong; their worried, glassy, yellow eyes looked around with a mixture of fear and accusation. We led one to a covered area behind the farmhouse – just outside the annex where I slept, I might add – where the concrete floor sloped towards a drain in the centre.

The sheep bowed its head, bleated and shuffled backwards. I pulled it forwards and held it still so that Jacques-Henri could thwack it squarely on the back of the skull with a hammer. I held my breath. Crack! The sheep fell to the floor, apparently stunned but with its eyes wide open and spasms running through its muscles. I cringed. Jacques-Henri explained that there was a particular spot to hit just where the skull joined the neck, so that the hammer blow would paralyse and numb the animal. I don't know if this really spared the sheep from feeling any pain; in the circumstances I had to believe him.

We fitted a hinged iron ring to the end of a long chain, then closed it around the sheep's hind legs. A pulley was attached to a beam in the roof directly above the drain. We looped the chain over the pulley and I hauled on the other end to raise the sheep up, so that it hung by its back legs. Jacques-Henri took a long knife and stabbed the sheep through the throat. It twitched slightly as he twisted the knife to open a hole wide enough to let the blood gush out. The blood drenched the animal's head and gurgled, thick and red, down into the drain below. After about a minute the flow abated, just a few gooey drops fell, the twitching stopped, the life of the sheep was ebbing away. It was startling for me to see an animal die like this for the first time.

I rolled a wheelbarrow under the sheep and held the body steady, while Jacques-Henri slit it open along its belly. Working fast he disembowelled it, letting the intestinal sack fall, with a plop and a squelch, into the wheelbarrow. He took care not to let the intestines touch the flesh of the sheep, which would have caused contamination. The intestines gave off a putrid stench that made me retch; they were disposed of immediately, buried in a hole in the ground.

We lowered the sheep onto a table. Jacques-Henri hacked off the lower sections of its legs with a saw. He skinned the animal by expertly pushing his fists between its skin and its body. With the lower legs removed, the hide came off in one piece. He looked at his work with quiet satisfaction: to him it was just another job on the farm that had to be done. Jacques-Henri cared for his animals while they were alive. When the time came for them to be killed, he did it with speed, skill and the minimum of fuss.

We put the carcass in a big plastic bag, placed it in the freezer, and went back to the *bergerie* to get the second sheep.

Then I had to take a more active part. Jacques-Henri struck the animal on the back of the skull. Together we chained its hind legs and hung it up.

'*Vas-y*,' said Jacques-Henri, passing me the knife.

I stabbed it through the throat and twisted the knife. The razor-sharp butcher's blade moved surprisingly easily as I turned it. Jacques-Henri gave me a cloth to wipe the blood off my hands.

The farm brought me into contact with a natural order: I understood that killing had its place. Killing the sheep was a rite of passage. I had cut my teeth, as it were, and truly earned Jacques-Henri's respect.

Some sheep were sold for slaughter. We took them in the back of the old 2CV van to the abattoir at Boulogne-sur-Gesse. I'm sure they had an inkling of where they were going: they were restless and agitated, with an air of foreboding. The back of the van was like the condemned cell. We had to push them into the van at the farm and drag them out when we got to the abattoir.

'Do you know the old nursery rhyme about the sheep on its way to the butcher's?' Jacques-Henri asked me, as he slammed the back door of the van on the two sheep inside.

'No, I don't,' I replied. But I felt sure he was going to tell me.

> *Mouton, bê, où vas-tu?*
> *À la boucherie, perdre la vie.*
> *Mouton, bê, quand reviendras-tu?*
> *Jamais.*

> Sheep, baa, where are you going?
> To the butcher's where I shall lose my life.
> Sheep, baa, when will you return?
> Never.

Jacques-Henri told me that by guarding the sheep I was joining a long tradition of shepherdry in Gascony. 'You see those hills over there?' he said, pointing to the south. 'They are the winter grazing pastures for sheep brought down from the Pyrenees in the *transhumance*.'

'The *transhumance*?'

'Yes, the twice-yearly migration of mountain sheep,' Jacques-Henri explained. 'The sheep spend the summer on high pastures, the *estives*, eating fresh mountain grass. When the weather begins to turn bad, the shepherds lead them down to more sheltered lower hills, where they spend the winter, until the first mild days of spring give the signal to move the sheep back up to the mountains. The *transhumance* used to be a wonderful sight: hundreds of sheep moved in long lines, like rivers of grey wool flowing over the green, grassy slopes. The lead sheep stood out from the rest of the flock by the bells clanging around its neck and the brightly coloured pompoms bobbing on its head.

'Nowadays, the *transhumance* mostly takes place in lorries by road,' he added nostalgically. 'You rarely see such sights any more.'

Labrit

# MADAME PARLE-BEAUCOUP

'**M**artin, Bruno and I are going to the café. Want to come?' Paul asked, one Saturday.

'I didn't know there was one.'

'Of course there is. We'll show you.'

The three of us set off on foot into the village.

'We buy our tobacco at the café,' Paul said. 'The woman who runs the place is very nice, but she talks so much, we call her Madame Parle-Beaucoup.' Mrs Talk-a-Lot.

A big black-and-white dog barked at us excitedly from behind a wire fence in a garden. We were nearing the centre of the village.

'Here's the café,' said Paul, as we approached one of the houses on the main road. It had a rusty-red-painted iron porch overhanging the step and a large welcome mat outside. Otherwise there was no indication that this was a drinking establishment.

The café was in reality little more than someone's front room, with a bar along one side and a collection of tables, where the local men gathered to drink pastis and rough red wine. On this Saturday afternoon there were just a few regulars. Paul and Bruno shook hands with everyone and introduced me. The only decoration in the café was a rather dusty-looking boar's head mounted on the wall.

Two old regulars propped up the end of the bar. I was introduced to the shorter one in front first.

'Ah! Monsieur is English. Are you a 'ooligan?'

'No, I'm not a hooligan.'

His taller friend pushed him on the back of the shoulder. 'Does he look like it?'

'*Eh*. You never know with foreigners.'

I wasn't sure I liked being talked about like this.

'He is more like zee eeenglish gentleman,' said the plump woman behind the bar, who stood looking proprietorially over her customers. I presumed this was Madame Parle-Beaucoup. She wore a blue and pink flower-patterned apron-dress, and big, square glasses, like television screens.

Her intervention had the effect of shutting up the two old regulars at the end of the bar, and they got on with reading their shared copy of *La Dépêche du Midi*. Paul asked for a packet of tobacco and some cigarette papers.

Madame Parle-Beaucoup went behind the wrought-iron stand at the other end of the bar, which served as her tobacconist's cabin. The selection was limited: the only tobacco was Drum, in its familiar blue and red pouches; the papers were the cheapest brand, OCB; there were cheap French cigarettes, Gauloises and Gitanes, with and without filters; more expensive foreign cigarettes, Marlboro and Winston; and for the discerning smoker, packets of Reinita small cigars.

Madame Parle-Beaucoup lived up to her name. She talked very quickly, going on about life in Péguilhan. The French have a fondness for talking about their ailments, and Madame Parle-Beaucoup was like a walking, talking register of the state of health of the village. She knew in detail who was ill, who was getting better, who had a strong constitution, and who had irregular bowel movements and was always pestering the retired doctor next door. I felt I was learning more than I needed to know about the lives of the Péguilhanais.

She stopped talking only when a customer interrupted her. She had more time to chat when she did a round of the tables to collect empty glasses. Although she spent so much time talking, she also gave the impression of being always busy.

Madame Parle-Beaucoup's husband put in a brief appearance. He hardly said a word. I guess he would have been… Monsieur Parle-Très-Peu. Mr Talks-Very-Little.

Madame Parle-Beaucoup saw the Péguilhanais as an extension of her family, and anyone who was welcome in the café she thought of as part of that family too. She didn't speak to me any differently than she did the locals. Some of her information was useful, like when the baker's van or the grocer's van would be coming to the village, who I should ask for a lift into town, and even what to do if I had a problem with my bowels. Unlikely, I hoped!

Madame Parle-Beaucoup was very well meaning, but she did go on. We stood listening to her until our eyes watered.

'*C'est un vrai moulin à paroles!*' Paul exclaimed, as we made an overdue exit. She's a real word mill.

The black-and-white dog behind the fence barked at us as we passed, exactly as it had done on our way there. Then it stopped barking and returned to its kennel, satisfied that it had done its job and seen us off.

# FROM FIELD TO TABLE

M Y SENSE OF PLACE ASSOCIATED WITH THE LAND WAS deepening. Péguilhan lay in the heart of the area named the Comminges after the ancient tribe the Convenae. Hidden quietly away in southeast Gascony, the Comminges was described locally as *entre plaine et montagne*, between the lower hills of the plain of the Gers and the foothills of the Pyrenees. Its special charm was that it lay comfortably between extremes, neither too hilly nor too flat, neither too rugged nor too soft, neither too rich nor too barren, neither too arid nor too wet. The fields formed a varied patchwork of sunflowers, maize, wheat and pasture. Some fields were small, some swept out as far as the eye could see across a hillside or along a valley. The towns and villages lay far apart; the land rolled on, over open undulating hills, with only occasional signs of human habitation, until a church spire on a hill signalled the next cluster of houses. Travellers who headed for the more usual tourist destinations like the Gers missed the Comminges. The Gers was tourist Gascony, if you like, Gascony lite, while down here in the Comminges was no-compromise, full-fat, high-tar, Gitanes-*sans-filtre* Gascony.

The northern Europeans and other foreigners who ventured down to the Comminges were looking for escapism, for a world far removed from what they knew at home, slow paced, untouched by the trappings of modern tourism. By contrast, the French were looking for the roots of deep France, *la France profonde*, at the bottom of their own back garden, where the country ways were about rediscovery.

Péguilhan sat comfortably along an undulating hill-top. Woods surrounded most of the village on the slopes that rolled away from the backs of the houses. Looked at from a distance, the village and the hilltop seemed to embrace one another, as if they had grown together over the centuries.

One morning I set about cleaning the grill in the wall, where I would almost certainly be grilling *magrets de canard* later that day. I was shovelling out the dead charcoal ash when Jacques-Henri came out into the courtyard.

'Martin, there's a couple just arrived, they're in the hall. I think they're American, they don't speak French. Could you come and talk to them for me?'

'Of course, I'm coming,' I replied, feeling useful as an interpreter. I wiped the ash off my hands with a cloth and followed him through to the front hallway. I normally worked behind the scenes and had very little face-to-face contact with the guests, so this was a change.

The Americans were both slim and soberly dressed in navy-blue tops and khaki slacks.

'Hi there. You're British!' the man said, sounding upbeat.

'Yes. Where are you from?' I asked.

'We're from California,' they said together, confidently.

'We found this place just by accident,' the woman said.

'That's right,' her husband explained. 'We hired a car and have been exploring this part of France for a couple of weeks now.'

'This place looks very charming,' his wife went on. 'We'd gotten ourselves lost on these narrow roads when we saw the sign for the Auberge.'

'Well, I'm glad you found it,' I said, feeling more like the host than merely the interpreter.

All the while Jacques-Henri stood looking on, grinning broadly, not understanding a word that was being said.

'So how long have you been working here?' the man asked, a little surprised to come across an Englishman working in this far-flung corner of southwest France.

'A few weeks now, it's beginning to feel like home,' I replied.

'And what about your boss here,' the man asked me, 'is he good to work for?'

'Oh, certainly, always joking.'

Jacques-Henri decided it was about time he took charge of things again. In his favourite role of attentive host, he ushered us through to the restaurant. '*Venez, venez, asseyez-vous*,' he said warmly.

The Californians sat down at a table and looked at the menu. Then they turned to me. 'It's good you're here,' they confessed. 'We don't understand anything.'

'This is traditional Gascon country cooking, *la bonne bouffe gasconne*,' I explained. Good Gascon grub. 'Family recipes, home-grown produce from the farm. The animals are reared in the open air, fed on their mother's milk and on cereals grown on the farm. The fruit and vegetables are grown in the family's own garden and orchard, picked by hand. And of course, everything is organically produced. Trust me, I follow the food every step of the way from field to table. I picked some of the vegetables myself this very morning!'

They were impressed. I think I was selling it well. I heard Marie-Jeanne saying something in the kitchen and Anja came out to take their order.

It was a hot day and the couple ordered an *assiette gasconne* and a bottle of Côtes de Gascogne, the easy lunchtime choice.

The restaurant was the old front dining room of the Auberge. It was quite small, with only about twenty places. The tables were covered with red-and-white chequered Vichy cotton tablecloths. The simple country chairs had wicker seats. The tableware was thick earthenware, caramel brown, highly glazed, with a yellow floral motif. The room had panelled walls; there was one small window to the front and to the side long, shuttered French windows, hung with lace curtains. Scenes of Gascon life, along with some more contemporary paintings, were on the walls. Rustic pottery, copper pans and a pair of pointed wooden sabots stood on the stone mantelpiece. The décor created a *cadre authentique*, an atmosphere conducive to good eating.

'This is just so quaint,' the Californian woman said.

'What's the shield over the fireplace?' her husband asked.

I wasn't sure so I asked Jacques-Henri, who explained, leaving me to translate. 'That's the shield of Gascony.'

The shield was a blue-and-red quartered escutcheon, with two golden sheaves of wheat and two silver lions rampant. Jacques-Henri insisted I tell them that the wheat sheaves and lions showed what the Gascons famously do best: farming and fighting.

The Californians took their time over lunch. When they'd finished they asked about the postcards pinned to the wooden beam over the kitchen door. These were from visitors who'd written to say how much they'd enjoyed the food. Some cards were from France, others from Spain, the Netherlands, Germany and even one from Quebec. The words they used spoke volumes about the food: *appétissant… délicieux… succulent… saveurs extraordinaires… l'amour des saveurs*. One visitor had styled himself *un pèlerin-gastronome*, a foodie pilgrim. The collection showed how the Auberge was becoming a magnet for gourmets keen to taste real Gascon food.

'We'll send you a postcard when we get home,' the Californian man promised.

They genuinely wanted to talk to Jacques Henri, but were frustrated at not speaking his language.

Jacques-Henri and I – the *aubergiste* and his trusty interpreter – accompanied them outside. They thanked us for the hospitality.

'That was a quality experience, just what we'd been looking for,' the woman said, as they lingered on the step, reluctant to go.

'Maybe we'll come back some day,' her husband suggested.

They got into their hire car and drove slowly down the drive, pausing at the bottom to look back, raising their hands in a farewell salute.

'OK, back to work!' I said to myself, in English.

'*Eh?*' said Jacques-Henri, looking at me curiously.

'*Bon, au boulot!*' I translated what I'd just said into French. I went back to the courtyard to carry on cleaning out the grill.

Nicolas, who was home from school, had overheard the conversation with the Californians. Not used to hearing English spoken, he was fascinated. While I shovelled the ash, he started asking me questions.

'Monsieur Martin, they were Americans, weren't they?'

'Yes.'

'From New York?'

'No, from California.'

'Oh.'

Although Nicolas didn't watch much television, he followed an American police drama set in New York, dubbed into French. The yellow taxis, which form the backdrop to any New York street scene, had obviously caught his attention.

'Do they have yellow taxis in California?' he asked.

'Well, I think yellow taxis are more typical of New York,' I suggested.

'And do they have yellow taxis in London?' he asked

'No. London taxis are black.'

He thought hard for a moment, looking a little disappointed. 'Ah!'

# AMANDINE

JACQUES-HENRI WAS TURNING HIS FARM ORGANIC, ADAPTING new ideas about sustainability to fit in with his native wisdom about the countryside. For a Gascon farmer, organic farming represented a return to traditional methods rather than the introduction of new techniques. Going organic was another way of going back to nature. Jacques-Henri was only waiting for his coveted *agriculture biologique* certificate.

The *bergerie* was his model for his conversion to organic farming, where the transformation had been so convincing. The sheep did their droppings on the floor, and compacted them with their hooves to form a dense carpet. Jacques-Henri used to spray it regularly with chemicals to keep the smell down and shovelled it out every few weeks. Sometimes the stench was awful.

Two summers previously he had stopped treating the *bergerie* floor with chemicals, leaving it undisturbed for weeks. The smell became worse than it had ever been, but gradually nature took over, the sheep droppings began to compost steadily, the smell lessened and was replaced by a healthy hum, the same smell that had greeted me the first time I poked my nose in the *bergerie*. The barn was now a more natural place for the sheep to be. About every six months or so, when the cake of droppings reached about twenty centimetres, the floor was shovelled out. The organic droppings made useful manure.

We shovelled out the *bergerie* once during the summer. It was back-breaking work, but it was also strangely satisfying as I ran the shovel into the cake of droppings to cut a slice, then slid it underneath to bring out a nice, big, neat wedge, which I tipped into a wheelbarrow. Nicolas had a worse job, carrying the droppings in the wheelbarrow to the manure heap. He pulled a face as he pushed the barrow along. It was very heavy and wobbled precariously, and once it toppled over under the weight.

Most of the work on the farm was physically hard and the hours were long, but at the end of each day there was a great feeling of satisfaction. Gradually, as my body grew accustomed to the physical work, the initial aches and pains subsided and I felt invigorated and strong.

I was on a steady learning curve in animal husbandry. Jacques-Henri kept a small herd of about a dozen Gascon cows. *La vache gasconne* is silver-grey in colour, sturdy and square bodied. It has lyre-shaped horns, strong hooves for the hills and an obstinate temperament. The extremities of its ears, its muzzle and its tail are black tipped. Its lashes are long and pretty, to protect its eyes from the glare of the sun as well as keeping out the flies. Gascon cows were originally bred to pull carts or ploughs and provide milk. They have a naturally haughty look on their faces, and an attitude to match. They will stare challengingly at strangers, as if to say – *this is my field, what are you doing here?*

Gascon cows can predict the weather:

| | |
|---|---|
| *Corno pounchudo*, | Horns down, |
| *Tèrro henudo*. | Earth baked. |
| *Corno leuado*, | Horns up, |
| *Tèrro mouillado*. | Earth soaked. |

One of the older cows in Jacques-Henri's herd wore a traditional Pyrenean cowbell, hanging from its neck on a collar made from finely worked strips of ash wood. The lower slopes of the field were out of sight, and when the cows had ambled to the bottom of the hill the bell could be heard clonk-clonking as if from nowhere. What a strangely comforting sound!

*Donner aux vaches*. Feeding and watering the cows was a twice-daily routine. I stretched the hosepipe across the track from the barn to refill their galvanised drinking trough through the fence. While the trough was filling up, I took forkfuls of silage to the feeding bay some way into the field.

One cow was dominant. She was much bigger and bulkier than the others in the herd, and she was the only one with a name, Amandine. She had a calf, which she protected fiercely. She viewed everyone with suspicion, people and cows alike. At the drinking trough, she shouldered the others out of the way or gave them a prod with one of her horns, lowing bellicosely, until she and her calf had drunk their fill. The rest of the herd just had to wait their turn.

The first time I climbed over the gate into the field with a forkload of silage over my shoulder, Amandine was standing between me and the silage bay, and her calf was standing next to it.

Amandine and I squared up to each other. I didn't want to back down and wasn't going to be put off by this bovine bullying. But she was obstinate. She lowered her head the way cows do when they're angry or threatened. Her silver and black horns were pointing my way. I couldn't help but think for a moment that the horns were quite stylish, but this was not the time for aesthetics.

Amandine spread her front hooves menacingly. This did not look good. Half a tonne of horn-topped Gascon cow was more than I could handle.

'*Meuh*!' she bellowed.

I decided to let her have the last word and backed off, sitting on the fence until Amandine and her calf had moved off to another part of the field.

I told Jacques-Henri about Amandine, but he didn't think it was a problem at all. The next feeding time he came with me. Amandine was near the fence. He leaned over and scratched her head between the horns. Amandine liked it: she rolled her eyes and looked calm.

'You obviously have a way with cows!' I said to Jacques-Henri.

When I tried it, she ducked her head and stepped back. The issue between us was never resolved.

In a field behind the main barn was a Gascon bull called Nelson. He lived on his own in the field, out of sight of the cows, to make sure he behaved himself. He was a massive beast, muscular like an Art Deco sculpture, darker grey than the cows, of pure Gascon pedigree.

Nelson was regularly hired out for breeding. The breeding agent came with a trailer to take him off to cows in the area whose owners had booked his services. We set up temporary fencing in the farmyard to direct him from his field to the open trailer. Nelson was very cooperative, trotting purposefully up the ramp without having to be led; he obviously knew where he was going. The ring in his nose glinted in the sunlight. When he was safely inside the trailer he gave a short grunt to let us know he was ready. The agent closed up the ramp and Nelson went off on his mission.

While he was away siring sturdy Gascon offspring, Paul, Bruno and I took the opportunity to clean out his field. Nelson covered his field with big pats, which we shovelled away from time to time to give the grass a chance to breathe. I wondered how he produced so much mess when he only ate grass and silage!

It was a good job I'd swapped my espadrilles for working boots, because my feet were covered in dung. It stank.

'*Ça pue, uh!*' said Paul, sniggering.

The following day it was my turn to laugh at Paul. He had been on shepherd duty and I had been working at the Auberge. Driving in the 2CV to the farm, I met him on the road. He was looking around anxiously in all directions, shielding his eyes from the sun with his hand, scanning the far corners of the fields.

'What's the matter?' I asked.

'I've lost the sheep!' he said.

'What, all of them?'

'Yes.'

'How?'

'I took them out to the field, and then to save time I went back to water the tomatoes.'

'You took Labrit and Mizou with you?'

'Yes, I can't believe how stupid I was,' he said, angry with himself. 'When I came out to the field again, the entire flock had vanished.'

We drove back to the farm and jumped on the faded orange, bug-eyed, pug-nosed Renault tractor. Paul started it up, I sat on the side seat over the big rear wheel arch, and we drove down to the field where he had last seen the sheep. The old tractor was dangerous. The engine belched out a cloud of smoke each time Paul changed gear. He was scared the tractor might roll over sideways as it bounced over the steep, bumpy field. The small front wheel on the higher side left the ground a few times. I was more than a little concerned about this, as I clung for dear life to the low sidebars of my seat.

Labrit and Mizou flanked us higher up the field. We stopped at intervals, shouted and whistled into the woods, then listened for an ovine sound in response. Nothing!

We were starting to panic. Eventually, we heard bleating noises in the woods on the other side of the valley. The dogs raced to drive out the sheep. Woolly lumps began to emerge from the undergrowth and the flock reappeared. We pulled the clumsier animals from the bushes, rounded them all up and led them back to the *bergerie*. What a relief!

We counted the sheep as they ran through the entrance to the *bergerie*. The counting process was haphazard and so we couldn't be sure if we'd lost any. Assuming one or two would not be missed, we never said a word to anyone about what had happened.

# PATTES THE PAWS

ATTES WAS A STRAY THE FAMILY HAD TAKEN IN. HE WAS AN elegant, mild-mannered dog, light golden brown, with a magnificent fan tail, a kindly, dark brown face and huge paws, after which he was named. Pattes looked like a cross between a golden retriever and some other large breed. He was a gentle giant.

This lovable rogue had turned up at the Auberge a couple of weeks before I arrived. No one knew where he came from. Pattes never went to the farm, where the harsh regime would not have suited him, he always stayed in the softer environment of the Auberge. He slept outside, as animals do in the country. He made his bed under the staircase to the gallery around the court- yard. He'd obviously never been a farm dog, he must have been a family pet, and making his bed under the stairs was as close to living in a house as he could get. He didn't have any sense of the rhythms of work and would happily join us for company whatever we were doing. During the day he casually wandered in and out of the kitchen, and never seemed to learn that there were cer- tain places he was just not supposed to go. Time and time again he was told to get out of the kitchen. *Pattes – dehors!* Outside!

This dog seemed to respond to me more than to any- one else. I spoke to him in English sometimes, and won- dered if perhaps he'd been left by an English family and recognised the sounds of a familiar language.

'Do you speak *Godon*?' I asked him. He looked at me with his head on one side, like a perplexed old man. Not conclusive.

The sheepdogs Labrit and Mizou viewed Pattes with deep suspicion. To them he was an intruder and a threat. Labrit often growled quietly at Pattes when he wanted to remind him whose patch this was. Pattes, about twice the size of Labrit, politely tried to ignore him.

One day after lunch, Pattes was heard yelping desperately outside in the drive. Bruno and I ran to see what was wrong. We found him panic-stricken, writhing on his back, flailing, hitting at his muzzle with his paws. I held him and tried to calm him while Bruno looked into his mouth. A bone had got wedged across the inside of his upper jaw. Bruno prised open his jaws and flicked out the bone. Pattes was so relieved and immediately quietened down. I was impressed at Bruno's presence of mind.

One evening, I was about to grill *magrets* for some visiting Dutch connoisseurs of Gascon food. I took a couple of fresh *magrets* from the fridge. They looked lovely and plump on the plate, and they felt fleshy as I held them to score the fatty side with a knife. I put the plate on the low step wall behind me while I stoked the cinders to make the fire hot for grilling.

I heard Marie-Jeanne ordering Pattes out of the kitchen. '*Pattes – dehors*! *Écoute. Pattes – dehors*!' she repeated, until he got the message.

He trotted out into the courtyard and hovered around behind me, sniffing the air attentively. He could smell the meat. Suddenly, seeing my back was turned, he seized his chance, reared up on the edge of the table with his big front paws, snatched one of the *magrets* in his mouth and ran off with it! I saw this happen out of the corner of my eye. I threw down the fire tongs and ran after him through the passageway and out into the paddock. Pattes was so pleased with his prize he ran in leaps and bounds, making his escape along the ridge towards a distant field. I stopped running. There was no point in chasing him. Even if I caught up with him, what was I going to do with the meat? I hope he enjoyed his *magret* after all that.

Jacques-Henri explained to the waiting Dutch guests what had happened and apologised profusely for the delay. They thought it very amusing. I took another *magret* from the fridge and restoked the fire.

The Cazagnacs were not keen on the idea of taking in strays because their time was already stretched, but Pattes was so good natured and easy to have around they began to accept him as one of their own. Whatever home he'd lost, he'd found a new home at the Auberge. He loved to sprawl on the terrace in the rear courtyard, basking in the sunshine. Pattes the paws!

# CASSOULET AND CORNICHONS

TUESDAY WAS CASSOULET DAY AT THE AUBERGE. CASSOULET IS a classic dish, a generous family meal and the pride of Gascon cooking. It is named after the earthenware pot in which it is traditionally cooked. Some say the dish was created out of necessity during the Hundred Years War, when anything to hand was thrown into the pot. There are many different variations made throughout Gascony, and possibly as many different recipes for it as there are cooks. Marie-Jeanne's *cassoulet au confit* was her own take on a well-known theme.

The first stage of preparing a *cassoulet* took place the day before: gathering white haricot beans, the local large variety, *haricots tarbais*. The haricots formed the bulk of the dish. We would collect a generous basketful of haricot pods. Inside the beans were plump, creamy and mottled. They were soaked in water overnight to make them full and soft. On Tuesday morning Marie-Jeanne prepared the sauce, consisting of onions, garlic, tomatoes, carrots, herbs and stock. She deseeded the tomatoes by scooping out the centres and pushing the flesh through a sieve with a wooden spoon. Meat formed the basis of the flavours: pork spare ribs, ham, shoulder of lamb and whole Toulouse sausages. A few pieces of pork rind added to the flavour.

The *cassoulet* was cooked slowly in the huge *fait-tout* cast-iron stockpot throughout Tuesday afternoon. The smell always made me feel hungry. The French word *mijoter*, meaning a long, slow simmering, describes the process so aptly, evoking the gentle bubble of the stew and the intermittent rattle of the lid. Towards the end of the cooking, *confits de canard* and some chunks of the local black sausage were added. Finally, the *cassoulet* was transferred into earthenware serving dishes, a layer of breadcrumbs spread on top and each dish baked in the oven just long enough for the breadcrumbs to form delicious golden crusts. Marie-Jeanne's *cassoulet* was hearty, filling, smooth and thick, with a rich, gutsy, warm, gamey, country flavour. There is a homely, reassuring quality about *cassoulet*; it is truly satisfying. If I were a Gascon, I'm sure it would be my comfort food.

The meals we ate *en famille* usually echoed the food being served in the restaurant. On Tuesdays, several dishes of *cassoulet* would be prepared during the course of the day, some for the restaurant and some for us.

When haricots were not being used in a *cassoulet*, they were served plain with vegetables. I told the Cazagnacs that in England we eat something called baked beans, small haricots cooked in a sugary, starchy, tomato-flavoured sauce, sold in tins. My description met with contorted expressions of revulsion.

'I've heard of these baked beans,' Marie-Jeanne said, 'but I've never tasted them.'

She explained that the French cook something similar in the form of *haricots à la tomate*, which sounded so much more gastronomic. It occurred to me that baked beans are really a sort of simplified *cassoulet* without the meat, although it was best not to say so.

At lunchtimes the restaurant was busy with local farmers and tradesmen, sitting with tourists and guests. In the evenings it was full of local people and residential guests at the Auberge. I was surprised just how much time and hard work go into running a successful restaurant. Everything needed to be done at once and the pace had to be kept up all evening, until eventually things began to slow down as guests finished their meals and chatted over wine and an Armagnac *digestif*.

Marie-Jeanne was a marvellous cook. Just as Jacques-Henri was truly at home on the farm, she was at home in the kitchen. She was a steadying influence when we were rushed off our feet. A special quality about her, which I hadn't noticed at first, was the way she quietly showed concern for everyone's wellbeing.

The spirit of the restaurant was about capturing and presenting the true flavours of the region, *les saveurs des beaux terroirs gascons*. The word *terroir* is deeply significant, describing all the factors – the soil, the climate, the stock, the methods of cultivation, the cooking techniques and the character of the people – which combine to give the food its distinctive flavour. *Terroir* embraces the landscape, the sense of place, the history of what people have always done there, and evokes a connection with patterns of life that have evolved in harmony with the land.

Goose fat, *graisse d'oie*, and duck fat, *graisse de canard*, are the defining background flavours in most Gascon cooking, like butter in Normandy or olive oil in Provence. They give a rich flavour to meat and vegetables and are the traditional means of preserving food. Goose fat was great for improvising something quick and tasty, such as *quartous*, potatoes that were quartered, parboiled, then pan fried in a good ladleful of fat, tossed in roughly chopped garlic and parsley, and served hot and crispy.

Duck breasts are reserved for *magrets*, the thighs for *confit*. Cooked in its own fat, *confit* looks solid in preserving jars, but the meat has a velvety, flaky texture. *Petits pois* accompany *confit* very well. Smaller pieces of duck and goose are cooked and potted as *rillettes*. The smallest pieces of meat and anything else left over, known as *les parures*, are fried in very hot fat to make *fritons*, crunchy, appetising nibbles, particularly delicious still warm.

Anyone with vegetarian tendencies may feel uncomfortable in Gascony. The Gascons are proud of their farming traditions and take a healthy attitude to their animals, especially when it comes to eating every part – and I do mean every part – of the animals they have so carefully reared. Some guests, especially the locals, loved their veal tripe, wobbly, off-white chunks of honeycomb-patterned calf stomach – oh yes, fried in goose fat – and eaten with capers to sharpen the flavour. Not for the squeamish!

The Cazagnacs bought their ducks and geese from a specialist farm about fifteen kilometres away, at L'Isle-en-Dodon. Marie-Jeanne made the trip there every two or three weeks and a couple of times I went with her. A notice at the entrance to the farm promised *VOLAILLES – CANARDS GRAS – OIES*. Poultry – fat ducks – geese. The plump free-range ducks lived in large enclosures in the fields in front of the farm. Some had arranged their own freedom: they'd escaped from the enclosures and were waddling along the drive and around the barns. They quacked happily and ruffled their tails as they pecked at bits of food on the ground. They had no idea of their fate.

We walked up to the top field to see the geese. They had a large field, with lines of trees for shade in the day and a long arched shed for shelter at night. These were big geese, fully mature, ready for eating. As we approached they were curious and boldly came up to the fence to eye up the strangers. Their persistent squawking sounded almost human, as if they were trying to talk to us, but we couldn't quite catch what they were saying. Inside the shed the floor was covered with khaki-green *caca*, and a pungent smell wafted out of the door.

Gascony is the homeland of good country cooking. The food reflects a landscape that is simple and unadorned, created by generations who have worked the land with love. *Cassoulet* can be put in tins, *confit de canard* can be put in jars, *pâté de foie gras* can be put in pots, but the food is best savoured among people who know the land, sitting around a stone table in the open air, on a summer evening with a glass of wine, listening to the chatter of friendly voices. Gascony is known for *la douceur de vivre*, a place for taking it easy and enjoying simple pleasures. Good food, good wine, good company: *la bonne chère, le bon vin, la convivialité*.

The secret of Gascon cooking lies in its honest simplicity. There are no overriding tastes, no strong seasoning, no disguising sauces. Flavours blend together, complementing each other rather than competing for attention. Natural flavours are allowed to speak for themselves. A pork sausage tastes like a piece of pork and contains chunks of meat, more like pressed pork than the ground-up paste of mass-produced sausages. The colours of the food, from the beans to the jam, reflect those of the land, shades of golden brown running together, with nothing sharp or intrusive to spoil the harmony.

Marie-Jeanne baked most of the bread needed for the Auberge. She made a simple *pain paysan*, a small oval-shaped wholemeal loaf. Sometimes she made dark rye bread, *pain de seigle*, which was slightly bitter and I particularly liked. This was Gascony – there was never a *baguette* in sight!

Nothing was ever wasted. When bread went stale it was torn into chunks, rubbed with a garlic clove and salt, then roasted, dipped in oil and eaten hot.

The restaurant offered a variety of local cheeses. Marie-Jeanne wrote out a list of those available that week, which she pinned up on the restaurant wall, stating the name, location and in some cases the telephone number of the producer. Customers could order cheese by type, texture, maturity and whether it was sweet or dry, *doux* or *sec*, describing what they wanted to taste. I liked a mild, creamy ewe's milk cheese, with a subtle aftertaste of lamb on the bone.

Marie-Jeanne's *pièces de résistance* were her tarts, both savoury and sweet. One of her most delicious was ewe's milk cheese tart, *tarte au fromage de brebis*, with shallots and herbs in a crumbly pastry. The tart was baked gently, and came out of the oven at the moment when the top was just turning a buttery-yellow-brown colour. Ideally served warm as a starter, the delicate moist filling trembled on your fork and the warm, cheesy flavour immediately flooded your mouth. It was a little taste of heaven.

*Tarte maison* was Marie-Jeanne's tomato and onion tart. When a freshly cut slice was put on the plate, the juicy syrup from the tomatoes oozed over the sides. I stuck my finger into the little pink pool to taste the tomatoey-oniony syrup, which was both zesty and sweet.

The orchard at the farm supplied fresh fruit for plum tart, *tarte aux prunes*. The plums were baked on a thin *pâté sucrée* base. The *tarte aux prunes* came out of the oven smelling warm and tempting, a shining glaze covering the succulent fruit, darkened to lustrous purple, almost black, and just beginning to shrivel.

The orchard produced more plums than could be baked in tarts. Surplus fruit would be stewed, pulped, sieved and preserved as *pulpe de pruneaux*. The pulped prunes had an intense flavour, tangy, rich and thick, with the appearance of melting chocolate sauce and a hint of chocolate in the aftertaste.

Marie-Jeanne's signature dish was a local speciality dessert, *croustade aux pommes*. She peeled and diced apples, then left them to soak in Armagnac. When they were well soaked, the apple pieces were placed on flaky pastry disks, which were covered with apricot jam; a disk of flaky pastry was put over the top and the edges pressed together. Making the *croustades* called for considerable dexterity: the flaky pastry had to be rolled into sheets so thin Marie-Jeanne referred to it as *le voile de la mariée*, the bridal veil. Before putting the *croustades* in the oven she brushed the top with beaten egg, then baked them until the pastry rose in layers of crisp, golden leaves. The moment she took them out of the oven, she gave them an extra drizzling of Armagnac. This ran quickly over the surface of the pastry and spattered on the hot baking tray, giving off a sharp, alcoholic aroma.

Marie-Jeanne made large quantities of jam, most of it for sale in jars, on display on the hall table. She used local fruit: plum, apricot, peach and watermelon. Watermelons grown especially for jam are quite different to those grown just for eating: they have hard, light-coloured flesh. With nothing artificial added, all the different jams turned out a natural brown colour. They were thick textured and retained the strong flavour of the fruit. The jam was sold in big 1.5 kilogram jars, with squares of ecru linen tied over the top of the lid. I watched Marie-Jeanne in a quiet moment in the dining room, smiling to herself as she cut out the linen squares using pinking shears to give pretty zigzag edges. She was performing a labour of love.

We often ate a fruit salad of Quercy melons for dessert in the evening. They had lovely, sweet, perfumed, orange flesh, which left a natural syrup on the lips. Marie-Jeanne poured a twist of mountain lime blossom honey, *miel de montagne au tilleul*, over the melons. The sharp flavour of the lime countered the sweetness of the honey. Delicious. The same honey was also used to sweeten a tisane infusion, which we sipped as we relaxed in the courtyard at the end of the evening's work.

The pleasures of the table are central to Gascon life. The importance of food to the wellbeing of the people was understood by the southwest's most distinguished son: Henry IV, the first Bourbon King of France. When Henry was born in the Château at Pau in December 1553, his grandfather rubbed the infant prince's lips with the local sweet Jurançon wine to make him manly and vigorous, a true Gascon. As a boy young Henry was a free spirit: he ran barefoot with peasant children in the mountains and grew healthy and strong. When he became king, he helped to heal the enmities of the religious wars and brought peace and prosperity to the country. The key to his domestic policy was expressed in a simple wish: that every Frenchman should have a chicken for his pot on a Sunday.

In Gascony, and particularly in the Béarnais area around Pau, they think of Good King Henry as one of their own, *lou nouste Henric*, 'our Henry'. He is also known as *lou Gentilhome gascoun*, 'the gentleman of Gascony'. In an endearing piece of political spin, Henry said that the rest of France was annexed to Gascony, instead of the other way round.

I found working with food enjoyable, but some kitchen chores were very tedious, in particular peeling the *cornichons*. These baby gherkins have a subtler taste than a full-sized gherkin. They are great pickled, but first they have to be peeled. The phrase *éplucher les cornichons* still revives memories of sore fingers and a stiff neck. The problem was that they couldn't be peeled; rather, they had to be rubbed with a tea towel to remove the rough outer skin. They were very small, smaller than my little finger, making the rubbing fiddly and awkward. Sometimes we did them in their hundreds and what seemed like thousands. Florence didn't seem to mind rubbing the cornichons; in fact she actually seemed to like it. Fiddly and repetitive, it was similar to threading melon seeds.

Cordials, such as *sirop de menthe*, *sirop de grenadine* and *sirop de violette*, were kept on a high shelf in the kitchen, near the doorway. Marie-Jeanne had told us that the *sirop de violette* was the most expensive cordial, distilled from violet petals, a speciality of Toulouse. One frenetically busy evening in the restaurant, Anja became a little flustered, not helped by Nicolas acting up in the kitchen. Reaching for a bottle from the shelf, she knocked off the bottle of *sirop de violette*. It smashed to smithereens on the floor. The *sirop* made a sticky, violet puddle, oozing around the broken glass, and I have to say it smelled lovely, perfumed and slightly heady.

Anja was clearly embarrassed. I quickly fetched a dustpan, brush and mop and cleared up the mess – to be helpful, of course, not because I was trying to impress her. She seemed to appreciate my gesture. I still wasn't sure what Anja thought of me, she kept her feelings quite guarded, but I'd like to think this was the turning point.

*fait-tout*

# WHERE ARE THE
# BRAKES?

BOUT ONCE A FORTNIGHT THE CAZAGNACS WENT TO A
farmer's cooperative wholesale grocers on the out-
skirts of Saint-Gaudens, where they stocked up
with staple foodstuffs they couldn't produce themselves,
like flour, sugar, tea, coffee and huge quantities of natural
yoghurt. Saint-Gaudens was the main town for the area,
named after the Gascon martyr *Sent Gaudenç*. The locals
know the town as just Saint-Gau.

Apart from the necessary trips to Saint-Gau for gro-
ceries, to L'Isle-en-Dodon for ducks, to Boulogne-sur-
Gesse to go to the market or the abattoir, and to a local *fête*
on a Saturday night, our world was largely confined to the
Auberge, the village and the farm.

The Cazagnacs gave riding lessons to local children.
They kept eight horses, all various shades of brown: some
a light roan, some a chestnut sorrel, and a couple of big
mares that were dark chocolate with dark manes and tails.

The field to the side of the Auberge served as a paddock, ringed with a portable electric fence. I remember
the fence only too well. It was made from a bright orange
nylon tape with fine metal wires woven into it, carrying
the current. It was high voltage and low amperage, so it
would shock but not harm. The tape was wound on plastic reels and stretched between metal poles with insulated
hooks attached to them. With the current switched off the

arrangement of poles was easily changed, allowing the horses to be moved around the field in rotation, grazing one part after another.

I had been warned not to touch the fence when the current was switched on. Curiosity got the better of me; after all, it couldn't do me much harm, could it? Thud! The jolt made my brain thump against the inside of my skull and it felt as if my feet had left the ground. I didn't touch the tape a second time.

There was a covered area where the horses were kept in bad weather and where they would sleep when the nights became cooler later in the year. It was a low, open-sided barn, with hay containers attached to the wooden posts. The saddles, bridles, reins and stirrups were kept in the tack room, *la sellerie*, to the side of the Auberge.

The local children came in small groups, by arrangement, to ride the horses for a small fee. They were matched with horses according to their size, but were too young to ride on their own. Paul, Bruno and I ran alongside the horses, holding the bridles, as we went round and round the paddock in a wide circle. The horses would walk at first, then we encouraged them to break into a trot. As the pace quickened the ride provoked very different reactions in the children. Some grew frightened and wanted to get off, others became overexcited and wanted to go faster and faster, crying out *vite! vite!*, laughing and waving their feet in the stirrups. It was exhausting for those of us running alongside; we panted more than the horses. The riding lessons were a slightly anxious time for the mothers watching from the sidelines.

Sometimes we rode the horses ourselves. I'd never ridden before. The first time we went out I was given a medium-sized mare and we set off towards the valley of the river Gesse. None of us wore a riding hat, showing flagrant disregard for health and safety.

As we started to speed up, I wondered how I might stop if I wanted to. '*Où sont les freins? Où sont les freins?*' I shouted. Where are the brakes?

But I soon got the hang of riding. Lean to the left, the horse goes left. Lean to the right, the horse goes right. Pull on the reins, the horse slows down. Push the stirrups like imaginary brakes, the horse stops.

Paul led the way for our little posse, with Florence close behind him, then Bruno, then me, then Anja. We rode down into the valley of the Gesse, reaching the cascade in the river. Wild mint grew on the banks of the pool below the cascade. I caught faint wafts of the fresh smell of mint as the horses trampled it under their hooves. Leaving the clearing by the pool, we climbed the hill up the other side of the valley, where the terrain became rough. I clung on as my horse made little jumps over brambles and fallen tree trunks. The going grew steeper and the horses' movements became laboured as they puffed and snorted their way up the narrow, stony path. They struggled to keep their footing. Small stones came loose beneath their hooves and skittered down the path.

The ride was exhilarating. At the top of the path we emerged onto an open, grassy upland and sat there on horseback to take in the view. The mellow countryside rolled on and on in all directions, bathed in golden light. Before us, a field of ripening yellow sunflowers sloped down towards Boulogne-sur-Gesse. The town capped a low hill. The tiled rooves of the houses clustered around the high gothic spire of the church. In the distance, the mountains rose up in two stages. First the land rose up towards the dark, flattish ridge of the foothills, the *Piémont pyrénéen*, then behind the real mountains soared steeply in a second tier. Looming and majestic, the summits were indistinct in the purple-hued afternoon haze. The Pyrenees always seemed remote and inaccessible; the mountains were a distant presence, a place where hardworking farmers didn't go without time or good reason.

The Pyrenees have an ancient, mystical attraction. Their caves gave shelter from the cold during the Ice Age; their valleys provided good hunting and pasture as the ice retreated. Some of the earliest known art in the world was made in the Grotte de Gargas, a natural cave hidden in the forests covering the foothills. The strange prehistoric paintings, about thirty-five thousand years old, show hands with truncated fingers – some say mutilated, I'd prefer to think just folded – in outline on the cave walls. Gargas is a strange place, unsettling and chilly even in summer. The caves take their name from the giant Gargas who according to local folklore stalked the woods in the area. This mythical giant was the original for the sixteenth-century satirist François Rabelais's literary giant Gargantua. At least that's what the locals will tell you.

# ARE YOU VIKINGS?

ANJA AND I WERE GIVEN THE JOB OF PUTTING UP A SIGN AT the crossroads in the centre of the village, directing people to the Auberge. Jacques-Henri made the sign, a sheet of metal painted brown, with two wooden posts attached. The words FERME AUBERGE were spelled out in white hand-painted letters and an arrow pointed to the left, with a simple flower painted above the arrow.

We carried the sign between us through the village. Jacques-Henri had told us to position it on the grass embankment next to the *Mairie*, opposite the road coming from the next village of Mondilhan. Anja held the sign in place while I hammered the posts into the ground. The metal sheet clanged loudly with each blow. The ground was hard and it took some effort.

A council works van drew up on the opposite corner of the crossroads. A workman dressed in official light blue overalls got out and went round to the back of the van. He hauled out his toolbox and plonked it down on the ground. It was obviously heavy, and he rubbed the small of his back with both hands as he straightened up. From under his blue canvas cap he peered at us across the road, scrunching up his leathery, sunburnt face.

He walked towards us.

'Do you think he's going to tell us that we can't put up our sign here?' I asked Anja, out of the corner of my mouth.

'No, I don't think so, he's smiling.'

He'd come over to speak to us simply because we looked like strangers.

'*Vous êtes pas du cwaing, eh?*' he asked. You're not from around these parts. *Cwaing* for *coin*; his Gascon accent was very strong.

'No. We're here for the summer. We're working at the Auberge.' We pointed to the sign we'd just put up.

'Ah, the Auberge. And this is your sign. It's funny that. I've come to repair the road sign, that one there, for Boulogne-sur-Gesse. You can see it's hanging loose,' he explained, nodding over his shoulder.

He laughed, amused that we were all doing the same thing. 'Why have you come to work at the Auberge?'

'We've come to improve our French.'

'*Eh?*'

'Yes, it's good to come somewhere like this, somewhere rural and traditional... an authentic experience.'

'Haven't you come here to learn Gascon? Monsieur Fustignac up the road,' he gestured up the hill, 'he only speaks Gascon. Of course, he can speak French if he has to, but he doesn't like to.'

'Really? No, we haven't come to learn Gascon, we've come to learn French.'

'So you're not French?'

'No.'

There was a pause. We began to realise we were talking at cross-purposes. The sign fixer hadn't grasped that not only were we not from the area, we were not even from France. In his mind there seemed to be only two languages in the world: Gascon and French. He thought the problem through, however, and rapidly widened linguistic horizons.

'If you want to learn French, why have you come here?' he asked with a hint of irony. 'You should have gone somewhere where they speak proper French.'

We had no answer to this.

He studied us thoughtfully for a moment, then asked suspiciously, 'Are you Vikings?'

I think he was joking. We assured him we weren't.

The sign fixer was very friendly towards his Nordic invaders. He knew the Cazagnacs and remarked that the food at the Auberge was getting a good reputation in the area.

Anja had her camera with her, so we asked the man to take a photograph of us. I still have a copy of the picture, showing Anja and me laughing, leaning on the sign. Behind us, an old stone barn with a red tiled roof squats beneath an achingly blue sky. Tiny white flowers on the embankment by Anja's feet mirror the flower on the sign.

The council workman finished his job, bade us farewell and set off in his van. His apparently random question about Vikings may have had some reasoning behind it. The Gascon collective memory has Viking pillage and plunder etched into its darkest recesses. In the latter half of the ninth century the Vikings raided Gascony nearly every year, sacking and depopulating every town they reached. They sailed up the river Gironde and attacked Bordeaux, then sailed up the river Adour to attack Bayonne, Dax, Aire-sur-l'Adour, Eauze and Condom. They made their way up the Gave d'Oloron and so completely destroyed the town of Oloron-Sainte-Marie that it took two centuries to recover. It was not until the year 982 that Duke Guilhem-Sans of Gascony assembled a force sufficiently strong to turn the Vikings away for ever.

When Anja and I had finished erecting our sign, we walked across the road to check that it was straight. As we stood admiring our handiwork, Hans and Lotte drove slowly by in their big old olive-green Mercedes-Benz 500 SEL. They were quite a feature around Péguilhan and we'd seen them often but never actually spoken to them.

It was such a small village that everyone naturally talked to whomever they happened to meet, especially strangers. Seeing us there, Hans and Lotte stopped the car and got out to talk.

'*Salut! Ça va?*' said Hans.

'It's so lovely and peaceful here, *n'est-ce pas?*' said Lotte.

They knew who we were, they wanted to speak to us because we were foreigners in the village. Hans and Lotte were German and lived in a pretty, pastel-blue house near the *Mairie*. They were in their forties. Hans had a sandy beard; Lotte wore a pale blue embroidered headscarf. They exchanged a few words of German with Anja, as a sort of confirmation, then they reverted to French. They told us how they'd escaped from the rat race in Frankfurt and were now living the good life under the Gascon sun. They made us promise that we would call in on them for lunch the following day. *Demain, c'est promis*. We happily agreed, and they got back in their car.

Hans and Lotte looked like upmarket hippies. The Mercedes was a relic from their former life and gave their new existence an air of genteel poverty. The car was getting old, but it ran smoothly, its huge engine purring beautifully.

It was time for us to go back to the Auberge. We walked round the bend in the road, past the long, crumbling wall in front of the château. Just down the hill stood a derelict house, an empty shell with no roof. It clearly had once been an elegant and formal residence: the stone around the doors and windows was finely carved and, judging by the tall windows, the ceilings had once been high. The plaster on the walls was cracked and broken and had been bleached by the sun.

We stepped gingerly into the courtyard. A small grey-brown lizard scurried up the wall and disappeared into the rusting iron frame of a window grille. The dilapidated walls were surrounded by an overgrown mass of brambles. We could see clusters of blackberries that looked as though they were nearly ripe.

'I want to pick some berries,' said Anja, 'to see if they're ready to eat.'

'OK.'

The nearest berries were far in among the brambles.

'I can't reach,' she said. 'Could you stand behind me and hold me by the waist while I lean in?'

This was an offer I couldn't refuse. I held her hips while she leant over the brambles and picked a small handful of fruit. Anja turned round. We were standing very close. She held a blackberry to my mouth for me to take a bite.

'Here,' she said.

I bit off half the berry.

She put the other half in her mouth. 'Yuck.'

The berry tasted sour, it wasn't ripe. Anja tossed the other berries back into the brambles.

'Never mind.'

We paused and looked at each other. We almost kissed – almost, but this wasn't the moment. We turned to leave, and abandoning the ruin, we walked back to the Auberge, in no hurry.

# HANS AND LOTTE

JACQUES-HENRI WAS GRUMBLING. A NEW OIL STORAGE TANK was needed for the Auberge, but it was going to be expensive. The old one was going rusty. It had already been patched up with welded panels, but might leak again before long and would have to be replaced. Jacques-Henri was looking through the catalogues. The world of oil storage tanks, *cuves à mazout*, looked very complicated. There were different types, in different shapes and sizes, *ondulée*, *cylindrique*, *rectangulaire*, and an array of different specifications. It looked as though he was going to continue grumbling about the oil tank situation throughout lunch. Fortunately, Anja and I had our date with Hans and Lotte.

We walked through the village. Most of the houses were spread out along the one main road. Many were very old. Built of stone in a similar style to the Auberge, each was set behind an enclosed front garden, with a gate in the front wall. The gardens were given over to vegetables growing in tidy rows: runner beans, courgettes, tomatoes, onions, celery, lentils… There were very few flowers. Every strip of land was put to some use. Several of the bigger houses were quite imposing, with elaborate iron railings along the front wall and arched doorways with fanlights. One house at the crossroads had an arched window in its wall, right on the road, set up as a shrine, with a statue of the Virgin dressed in a pale blue robe, raising a beatific hand.

Turning the corner by the *Mairie*, we recognised Hans and Lotte's big blue house. Their home was charmingly eccentric. The large front garden was full of different kinds of vegetables. The name of the house, Les Rossignols, was hand carved into a wooden sign by the garden gate. A rusty old bicycle stood by the gate, the basket on the handlebars used as a flower container. Flowerpots painted bright yellow and green were attached to the front of the house.

Hans and Lotte were sitting at their outdoor dining table. It was made from old shop signs bolted together and stood in the middle of the vegetable garden, in front of a line of tall, thistly-looking globe artichokes. The couple waved when they saw us walk up. Entering their garden was like stepping into an enchanted world. A calmness prevailed within the tumbling confusion of vegetables, flowers and makeshift furniture.

We sat on chairs that were in fact old wine barrels with a section cut out to form a seat.

Lunch was simple fare, starting with boiled artichoke hearts, still warm, for us to pull apart with our fingers and dip in oil, and a main course of *choucroute* and *saucisse de Toulouse*.

'We've been living here for, er, let me think, six years now, or is it seven?' said Hans, vaguely. 'We've never looked back. Life in Frankfurt was so stressful. Life here is so self-contained.'

'They're very good at keeping things hidden in these parts,' said Lotte. 'There's a lot more going on than you think.'

Village gossip! Hans and Lotte were incomers, they would tell us things the natives would never let out.

'You know the plump woman who runs the café?' asked Hans.

'Madame Parle-Beaucoup?' I replied.

'Well, that's not her name, but I see what you mean,' said Hans, amused.

'Go on,' I insisted.

'Well, you know she has a liaison.'

'You're kidding!' I said.

'Who with?' asked Anja.

'An elderly widower from the village,' said Hans.

'Monsieur Fustignac,' added Lotte, giggling at the thought.

'Oh, we've heard of him,' said Anja, 'he's the Gascon speaker.'

'That's right,' said Hans.

'Isn't Madame Parle-Beaucoup married?' I asked.

'Yes, she is married, but her husband turns a blind eye,' said Lotte. 'They have an understanding.'

'That Monsieur Fustignac, he has a reputation as a old womaniser, *un vieux trousseur de jupons*,' said Hans. 'Not bad for his age,' he added, with just a hint of scepticism.

Never having seen the infamous Monsieur Fustignac, we were not in a position to judge. *Trousseur de jupons* is a funny expression, literally a bundler-up of petticoats.

'They were caught once, *en flagrant délit*, in the *Mairie!*' Hans told us.

'It doesn't seem to have cooled his ardour,' laughed Lotte.

'A word of advice,' said Hans, in the tone of a friendly uncle. 'Always show the people here that you respect them, never let them think you're looking down at them. They're quite sensitive. The Gascons haven't always been treated well by outsiders. They've never forgiven Napoleon for conscripting a whole generation of young farmers into the army. They had riots over it at the time.'

We left knowing a lot more about Péguilhan than we had before lunch. One thing we'd learnt: there was more to the Péguilhanais than met the eye!

As we walked back to the Auberge we looked at the village houses in a different light, wondering what goings-on might be concealed behind those solid old wooden doors and shuttered windows.

# WHITE HORSES

ANJA AND I DECIDED NOT TO HAVE A SIESTE AFTER LUNCH. Instead, we walked out along the ridge of the hill to the west of the Auberge, away from the village. At the far end of the ridge where the ground fell away on three sides, we found a good vantage point with a beautiful view, and lay down on the grass. A thin line of trees gave some shade from the burning sun. In a field on top of the opposite hill, a pair of white horses grazed.

Anja had some letters to write. She lay on her front, letting her hair fall over her face for shade. While she wrote, I stretched out on my back and rested my arm over my face to shield my eyes from the strong light. The ground on the hilltop was baked hard, the parched grass dry and prickly. Wild teasels stood tall along the edge of the field, their spiny oval heads catching the light, glowing like small halos.

Anja finished writing her letters, sealed the envelopes and we started to talk. Anja told me how she liked to practise modern dance in her spare time.

'You'll have to show me some moves,' I suggested.

'Not here!' Anja replied emphatically, but flattered, I think.

Away from everyone else, we could say what we liked. 'What do you really think of life here?' I asked her.

'It's good,' she said, 'but don't you feel as if we've gone through a time warp?'

'Yes, we've gone back to the Middle Ages.'

'How do we explain the electricity and the running water?' asked Anja.

'Witchcraft.'

'Do you think Jacques-Henri is a wizard?'

'You never know!'

The conversation grew slower and more punctuated with pauses. We were only pretending to complain about things; it gave us an easy excuse to get a little closer.

All was quiet. The birds had taken shelter in the trees from the afternoon heat. Even the insects had fallen silent.

Suddenly, the peace was shattered by the sound of a fighter plane roaring overhead. *Bwwwcrcrcrcr...* The jet flew low over the hills then vanished into the blue, leaving a booming echo reverberating along the valley. All went quiet again. The two white horses on the opposite hill were startled and they galloped in a circle around their high open field.

'Ah, the twentieth century!' Anja and I both sighed at the same time, as we looked towards the spot where the plane had vanished. But the sky was empty, and we turned our attention to each other again.

Anja's skin was a sun-kissed honey colour, irresistibly touchable; the sun had brought out the sprinklings of freckles on the sides of her nose. Her purple t-shirt had little flakes of dry grass clinging to it. I edged a little closer and rested a finger in the dimple inside her elbow. Tiny silver-blonde hairs stood up on her forearm.

Over Anja's shoulder, in the distance, I noticed the two white horses on the opposite hill approach each other, brush their muzzles together, then continue grazing.

'Look at the horses over there,' I said, 'they're horse-kissing.'

'Are you suggesting we should do the same?' asked Anja.

'Well, we might…'

This was our moment. Taking our cue from the horses we kissed, tentatively at first, our lips dry in the afternoon heat, then more urgently. We breathed in each other's excitement, charged with a tingle and a spark.

It felt as if we were the only two people alive in the world, on that remote, sun-baked hilltop, in the dry, fading heat of the late afternoon. We lost all sense of time. Sooner or later we would have to return to the Auberge; the others would be wondering what had happened to us.

We walked as slowly as possible, sauntering arm in arm through the cool passageway into the courtyard, where Jacques-Henri was cleaning out the grill in the alcove. He stopped what he was doing, looked us up and down and smirked.

'*Ça va, les amoureux*?' he asked, cheekily. He did not look at all surprised to see us together.

# MÉCHOUI

A SUBTLE MOORISH INFLUENCE CAN BE FELT IN GASCONY, A North African connection that can be traced back a long way. Following their conquest of Spain the Moors, under General Abd el-Rahmann, made incursions into southwest France during the eighth century. They got as far north as Poitiers, where in AD 732 they were defeated by the Frankish army under Charles Martel. As the routed Moorish army retreated southwards, which took several years, some soldiers chose to settle in Gascony. Their presence remains hidden in place names such as Maurs, Mauran, Montmaurin, Puymaurin, Castelmoron and Castelsarrasin. The Gascon expression for getting a suntan is *hè's moret*, meaning to make oneself a little Moor. The Moors left some of their horses, which took refuge in the swamps and marshes of the Landes. Their wild descendants resemble modern Arab horses. The Moorish influence can also be seen in the architecture of some old brick churches. Perhaps their most enduring legacy in Gascony was the white bean they imported, ancestor of the haricot.

Bastille Day – *le 14 juillet*, the national day of the French Republic – was celebrated by the Cazagnac family with a small feast at the Auberge. The food showed influences from North Africa. The centrepiece was a *méchoui*, a North African celebration dish, a whole lamb roasted on a spit outdoors from morning through until evening. Jacques-Henri's younger sister Angeline and her husband

Bernard came to eat, along with a few invited locals, including Hans and Lotte and Monsieur Fustignac. Apparently no feast was complete without the one and only Monsieur Fustignac.

We all got up early on the morning of the *méchoui*. A suitably plump lamb had been chosen and slaughtered the day before. On the open ground beside the Auberge, Paul and I dug a trench about a lamb's length and a spade's depth. We scraped away the grass from around the edges, then filled the trench with firewood and stuffed in some straw kindling, which we set alight. By about mid-morning the wood was reduced to a glowing heap, with little flames dancing about here and there. At each end we set up an iron pole with a pivot and a ratchet at the top, which allowed the lamb to be slowly rotated and held in place at various stages of turning.

Jacques-Henri arrived with the lamb carcass. He was accompanied by a Moroccan man named Youssef, the local *méchoui* expert, who had come to supervise the start of the roasting. The lamb was placed on a makeshift table. Youssef and Jacques-Henri skewered it from end to end with a rotisserie spit. They stuffed the carcass with garlic, mint, seasoning, handfuls of butter, and hot Moroccan *harissa* chilli paste. I had a taste of the *harissa*, which had a real kick to it: at first it was mouth-puckeringly hot, then the heat softened into a warm, pleasing afterglow. Youssef brushed the whole body of the lamb with butter and lemon juice, then he and Jacques-Henri mounted the spit on the poles over the smouldering trench. As it began to roast, Youssef, with a practised hand, basted the lamb again with oil, butter and lemon juice. Jacques-Henri looked pleased that everything was in place and he went off to see to other things.

Paul turned the spit while I stoked the charcoal. Youssef explained that a *méchoui* is usually a celebration dish in his country. '*Dans mon pays, le méchoui c'est pour-r-r les gr-r-randes fêtes,*' he said, with the rich rolling *r* of a Moroccan accent.

We were going to have couscous and spiced vegetables with the meat. Youssef told us that couscous symbolises the act of giving. With a crinkly smile, he rubbed his thumb and fingers together as if to show grains of couscous running through his fingers.

Youssef left us with strict instructions that the lamb was to be rotated a quarter of a turn every quarter of an hour, until just before dinner, when it should be removed from the fire and left to rest. This meant that someone had to stay with the *méchoui* all day. We took turns on *méchoui* watch, Paul volunteering for the first shift.

I went back to the kitchen. Marie-Jeanne told me Jacques-Henri had phoned to say I was needed for shepherd duty at the farm. Both the 2CV and the Renault were already there, so I had to borrow Nicolas's *mobylette*. I'd never ridden one of these small, underpowered mopeds so loved by generations of French teenagers. I got on, kicked the starting pedal to get the tiny two-stroke engine going, pulled the throttle and rode cautiously for a few metres. I turned sharply on the gravel at the corner of the drive, the *mobylette* slid from under me and I found myself on the ground. I got just a few light scratches on my left knee and elbow, which smarted a little but were nothing too serious, so I dusted myself down and got back on. I said to myself – *if Nicolas can ride to school on one of these machines every day, then I can ride it too!* I set off again, carefully at first, then speeded up, riding all the way to the farm without falling off. The warm wind blew in my face, the countryside slipped by on either side, the air was redolent with the delicious smell of freshly cut wheatfields, and the *mobylette*'s tiny engine buzzed like a friendly wasp – it was easy to ride after all.

Back at the Auberge in the afternoon, Marie-Jeanne was preparing the couscous and spiced vegetables. I went out to the *méchoui* to take over from Nicolas, who was on spit-turning duty. Marie-Jeanne wasn't sure he was responsible enough to look after the fire on his own. I found him whittling on a stick. He gestured towards the lamb and made a surprisingly gourmand observation.

'Ça sent bon, eh, les épices?' he asked.

I agreed the spices smelled good, *appétissantes*.

Nicolas poked at the fire with his newly sharpened stick to harden the point, and accidentally took a flurry of hot smoke in the face.

The little yellow dog Rôti hovered nearby, licking his lips and looking for the slightest opportunity to get at the meat. He went right up to the edge of the trench, and with his head on one side and his tongue lolling, looked longingly at the *méchoui*. Rôti got so close to the smouldering charcoal he was lucky not to live up to his name.

Nicolas and I sat down on the ground, both of us staring at the lamb, now stiffened in its posture on the spit, after hours roasting, browning and blackening in parts. Nicolas stoked the fire again, this time more cautiously. There was a long pause, then he cleared his throat and adopted a manly posture, with his shoulders square and his fists on his knees.

'Well then, Monsieur Martin,' he said, as if he was about to say something important.

This was obviously going to be a man-to-man conversation. I squirmed a little, uncomfortable at the thought of what might be coming. He told me that he liked living on the farm, but it could get lonely.

'It's good to be a shepherd,' he confessed, 'but it would be better if there was a pretty little shepherdess for company.'

Poor Nicolas!

'*Faire goulou-goulou*,' he added.

'*Goulou-goulou*?'

'*Goulou-goulou*,' he repeated, laughing cheekily now.

In the local parlance *faire goulou-goulou* meant... er, just what it sounded like.

Guests started arriving in the evening, before the *méchoui* was ready but later than expected. They call it *le quart d'heure gascon*, the Gascon quarter of an hour. Gascons are habitually fifteen minutes late, and fifteen minutes can turn into half an hour or longer. Living the good life is more important than arriving on time. In Gascony the world turns slowly and people do things in their own time. The pace of life and the rate of progress are a little out of step with the rest of France.

Angeline and her husband Bernard arrived by car. They lived on a farm seven villages away, as distances were measured in those parts. There was a clear family resemblance between Jacques-Henri and his sister. Angeline and Bernard greeted each of us in turn. Men and women did the *bise* on both cheeks, which was quite formal etiquette for these people, for whom a handshake normally sufficed.

Hans and Lotte rolled up in their Mercedes. The big car always made its presence felt. Lotte opened the boot and brought out a present for Marie-Jeanne, a dried flower arrangement, stuck into an artichoke head used as the base. It was an unusual present, but typical of Lotte.

Paul looked up the drive. '*C'est Monsieur Fustignac qui arrive!*' he said. Monsieur Fustignac is coming – I was going to meet him at last.

Monsieur Fustignac had walked to the Auberge from his farm on the other side of the village. He looked exactly how I thought he would. His age was beyond guessing. He was wearing a brown double-breasted suit, which I would say was just post-war. He wore white spats over his shoes and a floppy beret on his head. His handlebar moustaches were well waxed into pointed tips. He thought he looked dapper. I thought he looked like a rustic Hercule Poirot.

We all sat round the stone table in the courtyard, waiting expectantly for the *méchoui* to arrive. Jacques-Henri and Paul appeared, proudly carrying the spit between them with the roast lamb hanging from it. They set up the poles again in the ground near the end of the table and remounted the spit.

Chair legs scraped on the gravel floor as people sat back out of the way. The roast lamb was still steaming slightly, dripping drops of juice, and it smelled delicious. Jacques-Henri sharpened his knife on his butcher's steel and began to carve the tender, succulent flesh. He relished being the centre of attention as he tossed the wedges of lamb onto a giant black-enamelled metal dish on the table. When the dish was piled high with lamb, he wiped his hands on a clean tea towel, then took a bunch of coriander leaves, tore them apart roughly with his fingers and sprinkled them liberally over the meat.

Down the steps from the kitchen came a small procession, first Anja and Florence each carrying a big blue-and-white glazed ceramic tureen of spiced vegetables, followed by Marie-Jeanne carrying a great big dish piled high with steaming couscous, done to perfection, neither too crumbly nor too moist, softened with a dash of oil. They placed the couscous and vegetables in the middle of the table and removed the lids. Jacques-Henri brought out a crate of Brut de Monluc sparkling wine and started popping the corks. Marie-Jeanne, radiant with pride, stood back to admire the feast on offer.

'Everything is ready,' she said.

'*Je m'en lèche les babines*,' said Jacques-Henri. I'm licking my chops.

The *méchoui* was ready for everyone to help themselves and the feasting got underway. A bowl of flame-red *harissa* was passed round the table for everyone to take as much of the fiery condiment as they dared.

I found myself sitting next to Monsieur Fustignac.

'I hear you speak Gascon?' I inquired.

'I am a Gascon and I speak Gascon,' he said, proudly. 'And you, do you know any Gascon?'

'No, although I've learned a few words, for herding the sheep.'

'You must learn some more,' he said, with conviction.

'OK, I'm listening.'

'*Adishatz*,' he said. 'That means hello and goodbye.'

'Just one word for both? That's quite simple.'

'Oh yes, we're a simple people,' he laughed.

As my lesson with Monsieur Fustignac continued, I found I had to make an effort with my mouth to mimic the sounds he was making. Hearing Gascon spoken, sonorous and full, the southwest French accent that I'd found so difficult to understand at first seemed to make sense – this was where it came from. Monsieur Fustignac told me that the Gascon tongue had grown out of the meeting of the old tribal language of the mountains with the Latin of post-Roman Aquitaine. It was important, he said, to prevent it from disappearing altogether. Speaking Gascon for him was an act of defiance.

Monsieur Fustignac raised his glass to me in a toast. '*A la toa!*'

'*A la toa!*' I repeated, clinking glasses.

As he drank, the rim of his glass pushed up the tips of his moustaches into a pointy smile. 'Have you heard of the *sarri*?' he asked me, very earnestly.

'No.'

'It's the antelope that lives in the Pyrenees,' he said. 'The *sarri* has legs on one side longer than the legs on the other side, so it can walk on the mountainsides, but it can only ever go round and round the mountain in the same direction. The male *sarris* have longer legs on the right side, the females have longer legs on the left. They meet each other once each time they go round the mountain.'

'But you must be joking,' I protested.

'I swear to you it's the truth,' he said, holding up his hands and making a wide-eyed expression of honesty. Under his beret, his old man's eyes looked watery. I knew he was winding me up, but he made it sound so plausible. With a few more glasses of Brut de Monluc inside me I might have believed him.

The *sarri* really exists: it is to the Pyrenees what the chamois antelope is to the Alps. In English it is called an izard. It looks rather like a goat, though it is not lopsided as Monsieur Fustignac described.

The thought occurred to me afterwards that he might have been trying to tell me something about men and women, but the meaning, if there was one, was too obscure for me to fathom.

While Monsieur Fustignac was telling me tales of strange animals Hans looked over at me, raising a questioning eyebrow, as if to say – *well then, what do you think of the old rogue?* I didn't make any reply, in case Monsieur Fustignac noticed. Besides, it didn't seem fair, the widower was there on his own. His paramour Madame Parle-Beaucoup and her husband were celebrating *le 14 juillet* elsewhere.

Jacques Henri came round the table to talk to everyone in turn. He wanted to make sure all his guests felt at home. He'd drunk, as they say in Gascon, *un brave còp de vin* and he'd been chasing his wine with slugs of Armagnac, the mix of drinks making him ever more loquacious. He leaned heavily on people's shoulders at each stop on his way round.

Angeline and Bernard didn't have any children of their own. They were making a fuss of their nephew.

'Hasn't he grown, *le petit Nicolas*!' exclaimed Angeline.

'I am not *le petit*!' he objected, irritated. He was nearly fifteen.

Anja and Lotte were talking together in German; Anja was pleased to speak her own language for a change.

Paul and Florence, I noticed, were getting on very well.

Monsieur Fustignac stood up and proposed a toast to congratulate Jacques-Henri and Marie-Jeanne for such an excellent Bastille Day feast.

'*Bravo!*' said the whole table.

Jacques-Henri tried to look modest and thanked everyone for coming.

What was that I saw? Jacques-Henri giving Marie-Jeanne a peck on the cheek? This was the first public display of affection I'd seen between them.

There was an atmosphere of bonhomie around the stone table. Everyone chatted and relaxed. As the wine flowed, the conversations grew more animated. I noticed a change take place in people's bearings, their manner softening as the mantle of hard work gradually slipped from their shoulders. The warm day evolved into night; oil lamps were brought to the table and lit. In the lamplight faces glowed and eyes sparkled; we were all flushed and replete with wine and good food. I licked sweet, spicy lamb juices satisfyingly from my fingers.

The *méchoui* was an indulgent interlude, allowing us to gather our strength for the hardest work of the summer. It marked the beginning of the busiest period for the Auberge. As they say throughout France, *du 14 juillet au 15 août, c'est les vacances*! From Bastille Day to the Feast of the Assumption, it's holiday time. This was the time when most French visitors came to the Auberge, and Jacques-Henri was conscious of playing to a different audience.

# TOUR DE FRANCE

THE NEXT EVENT AFTER LE 14 JUILLET WAS THE TOUR DE France. That year the Tour passed along the main road in the valley a few kilometres to the south of Péguilhan. Anja and I were keen to see it and wanted to know the best place to watch. On the morning of the day the Tour was due, Jacques-Henri gave us a lift down to the main road, picked a good spot and left us there, saying he'd be back later in the afternoon. He'd seen the race before.

The road through the valley was long, flat and straight, a typical French road, shaded along both sides by lines of trees. We'd been dropped off near a small group of houses and barns by the road. We were the first to take our places on this empty stretch and it looked as though we were in for a long wait.

After a while, a few cars pulled off the road and people got out. The residents of the nearby houses set up picnic tables and chairs on the grass verge, preparing to enjoy the spectacle and make a family event of it. One family invited us to sit at their table and have a glass of wine with them. Monsieur was proud the Tour was coming along *his* road. For people who rarely travelled, the race brought a glimpse of the outside world. This was Stage 16 of the Tour, from Blagnac to Luz-Ardiden.

By the time the road had been closed off there were a few dozen spectators along our stretch. A gendarme came by to see order, casually pushing back his kepi with his thumb as he stopped to chat to us. Near where we were sitting we watched a man setting up his camera on a tripod, carefully positioning it to face the oncoming cyclists. There seemed to be a technical problem with the camera; he was becoming exasperated and swore under his breath, *espèce de*... His wife sat on the grass reading a book and taking no notice.

We'd been waiting there for well over two hours when we saw the publicity caravan approaching. We stood up and went to the edge of the road. A fleet of strangely shaped promotional vehicles sped towards us, advertising everything from soft drinks to financial services. With their lights flashing and klaxons blaring, for a few minutes they formed a bright and noisy cavalcade streaking along the valley. As they sped by, representatives of the official sponsor of the Tour, the French bank Crédit Lyonnais, threw out handfuls of badges for the spectators to pick up. We collected a few that landed on the road just in front of us. They were in the form of the yellow jersey of the Tour leader, bearing the bank's logo, CL, in blue.

The scale of the event was amazing. The support vehicles, plastered with multicoloured company slogans, carried spare bicycles in racks on the roof and on frames attached to the back. Serious-looking team officials sat inside. In their wake came television crews from all over the world, with elaborate outside broadcast equipment; then came the team cars; and then silence descended and there was a long, empty pause. We felt a sense of mounting expectation.

We knew the Tour itself was approaching when we saw the blue flashing lights of the motorcycle squad of the *Garde républicaine*, heading towards us in formation. They were wearing sharp blue uniforms, with gleaming white elbow-length gauntlets and white helmets. Each *motard* kept one hand resting nonchalantly on his hip as he rode his bike. The smart police motorcyclists reminded us that France was a land not just of farms and sheep, but also of ceremony and style.

There was a sense of excitement in the air as the world's greatest cycle race approached. Ahead of the cyclists came the referee watching the race through the open sunroof of his official car, marked *Direction générale*. Television cameramen, riding pillion on motorcycles, facing backwards, jostled for position to get the best pictures. When the cyclists finally came into sight, we heard a small boy nearby shout excitedly to his parents, '*Ils arrivent! Ils arrivent!*' They're coming!

The cyclists came by in three groups, first the small breakaway group, the *tête de la course*, followed a few seconds later by the main *peloton*, chased by the stragglers at the back. They passed at such speed we hardly saw a thing, just glimpses of suffering faces, straining sinews, shiny helmets and garishly coloured Lycra, accompanied by the fleeting whoosh of wheels. Spectators shouted support and whirled their rattles. Then it was all over, except for the following team cars and the rearguard of the motorcycle escort. We'd waited for over three hours in the hot sun to see about thirty seconds of cycling. The road was reopened and the people watching by the roadside began to disperse. There was a sense of anticlimax; we felt short-changed. We had no idea who we'd seen or in what order.

We didn't know what time Jacques-Henri would come to collect us. Noticing a huge log lying beside the lane that led off the main road, we went to sit on it and wait for him. The lane disappeared between fields of tall maize. A settlement of gypsy caravans stood on a piece of elevated ground. Their rooves were just visible over the thick green ears of maize. Some gypsies were moving about in the camp. We could hear their voices faintly, but we couldn't see them. I wondered what their life was like.

'Wouldn't it be exciting,' I said to Anja, 'to run away with the gypsies?'

'I don't think you'd like it,' she laughed, gently teasing. 'Besides, they don't accept outsiders very readily.'

She was probably right.

Rays of sunlight shone through the gaps between the maize stalks, slanting across the log where we were lazing, and motes of dust floated in the sunbeams. The maize gave off a dry, dusty odour.

Two gypsy women, one very old and the other much younger, suddenly appeared around the corner of the lane and walked towards us. We hadn't noticed them watching the race. As they approached, we heard them talking in a language we didn't understand, which could have been Romany. They were a striking pair, with an air of intensity. The old woman was small and thin, with a wizened face like a seasoned walnut, her thick grey hair tied back in a knot. The younger woman was much taller. She had a pinched, bony face with feline features, and watched us intently with yellow eyes that didn't miss a thing as they flickered between Anja and me. Speaking French with an accent that was thick and unfamiliar, the old woman did the talking for both of them.

'You're strangers round here, aren't you?' she asked. She fixed me with a penetrating stare and offered to read our palms for fifty francs. We were mesmerised and found it difficult to refuse.

It was Anja's turn first. The old gypsy woman took both of her hands by the fingertips, studied her palms for a few long seconds, brushed the fleshy mounds at the base of her thumbs, then looked her straight in the eye. She said some things about Anja that I couldn't hear, then it was my turn. When she'd finished, we crossed her palm with a 50 franc note.

Both gypsy women smiled, nodded, and walked on down the lane. They disappeared from view behind the maize as they turned the corner into their camp. Just then, from somewhere in the camp we heard the sound of a guitar strike up, strumming a *seguidilla*.

It's unlucky to repeat a gypsy's prophecy, but one thing she said I feel I can tell. 'This is a good time for you,' she said, 'and one day, when you've almost forgotten about me and this place, something you read in a newspaper will bring you back.'

# NO GRAIN, NO PAIN

WHEN THE TIME CAME FOR THE FIRST WHEAT HARVEST, Jacques-Henri told me we were going to winnow the grain and store it up in the loft in the barn. *On va monter du grain.* He warned me it would be tough work. No problem, I can do it, was my response. Was I acquiring that legendary Gascon overconfidence? Was this my first *gasconnade*?

The phrase *monter du grain* still makes me wince. It was one of the most physically unpleasant experiences I'd ever known.

Out in the fields the grain was harvested with a combine harvester, *la moissonneuse-batteuse*, which was owned collectively by the local farmers and employed on the farms in rotation. The harvested grain was loaded into a trailer and brought to the barn by tractor, where it was tipped in a heap on the floor.

The combine harvester had already threshed the grain, separating the wheat from the chaff. In the barn the grain was passed through a winnowing machine called a *vanneuse*, which cleaned the grain and removed the husks before it was stored in the loft. The *vanneuse* was a particularly nasty-looking piece of agricultural machinery. This model was very old. It looked battered and its red paint was chipped all over. A moveable steel pipe, about two metres long and fifteen centimetres in diameter, protruded from the body of the *vanneuse*, with a screw sticking out of the end.

We lowered the screw into the middle of the grain heap. Jacques-Henri cranked a handle on the side of the *vanneuse* to start it up. The noisy, petrol-driven contraption rattled, groaned and clanked, and the screw inside the steel pipe rotated rapidly, drawing up grain from the pile. The grain disappeared up the pipe into the main body of the *vanneuse*, where it passed through a series of grilles, which cleaned the grain before it entered an aerator that expelled the husks and other waste material. The winnowed wheat grain was pushed out of the other side of the machine into hoppers, which went up and over and down on a continuous conveyor, like a paternoster lift, tipping the grain one hopper at a time on the floor of the loft.

Jacques-Henri operated the machine while Paul, Bruno and I shovelled the grain from the edges of the pile towards the screw. It was gruelling work. We shovelled hard and fast to keep up with the rate at which the screw was drawing grain from the pile. The danger was only too real: get too close to the rotating screw and it would instantly take off a hand or half a foot.

'My ancestors would have done this by hand, you know!' shouted Jacques-Henri above the noise of the machine.

*Good for them*, I thought, really starting to suffer.

The *vanneuse* produced a fine, sharp dust that filled the air in the barn. We had to work with our tops off so the dust wouldn't get under our clothes, where it would scratch and sting. The fragments of wheat chaff were barely visible and they were viciously sharp. Taking off my shirt wasn't enough protection for me. The dust severely stung the whole surface of the skin on my upper body, as if I was being pricked with thousands of tiny

147

barbs. I desperately wanted to scratch myself, but doing so made it worse. Jacques-Henri, Paul and Bruno's bodies were hardened to the task, but my unseasoned skin couldn't bear it. The machine went on scraping and grinding; the dust made the air in the barn stifling and oppressive, and hurt my eyes and my nose. I tried to keep going, but the pain became unbearable. Eventually I couldn't stay in the barn any longer and I asked to be excused.

I walked outside to take a deep breath. Standing in the sunlight, I shuddered with the intensity of the stinging. I stood there with my arms held away from my sides, the sweat running down my back cruelly added a tickling sensation to the burning. Angry pink blotches appeared on my skin where I'd scratched it.

I went into the farmhouse and took a cold shower. Standing perfectly still under cold water, trying to get my breath back, I said to myself – *there's no need for this! I could pack up and leave now. I'm sure Anja would understand. Perhaps she would come with me?* Gradually the pain eased and my sense of reason returned. When I went back to the barn, Jacques-Henri, Paul and Bruno had finished the work. The grain pile had gone. I was worried about what they might think, but they recognised the discomfort I'd been in.

Jacques-Henri's only comment was a piece of wry understatement, '*Ça pique, eh?*' It stings.

I took part in winnowing again the following week and the experience wasn't much better. Although Jacques-Henri was firm about work, he was always fair-minded and he let me off all grain winnowing after that. Of the many and varied tasks that were thrown at me through the course of the summer, winnowing was the only one I couldn't hack and the only time I seriously questioned whether I wanted to stay. *Oh la vanneuse!*

# LE PERCHERON

JACQUES-HENRI WAS IN AN EXCEPTIONALLY GOOD MOOD. THE news had arrived in the post that the farm had been officially awarded organic status and could label its produce *de culture biologique*.

'All *stagiaires* can have the afternoon off!' he announced.

Anja and I decided to have a look at the events on the village noticeboard. Péguilhan's information point was a rather shabby wooden board attached to the wall next to the café, plastered with posters announcing forthcoming local events. A colourful poster advertised a concert to be given by a Pyrenean male voice choir, Les Chanteurs du Comminges. A picture of the Chanteurs showed a group of mature gentlemen, singing enthusiastically, dressed in red, white and black costumes, with big red bowties, red cummerbunds and floppy black berets. Nearby villages, Ciadoux, Escanecrabe and Nénigan, advertised their festivals. Musical notes dancing around on the posters gave notice of the entertainment to be expected: *DJ ANIMA-TION* and *DISCOMOBILE*.

We stopped to look in the small village church that stood right on the road. It was a simple, stone building, with small windows and a belfry with a short, square spire. A big wooden porch covered the area in front of the door, which was unlocked during the day for anyone to walk in. I lifted the heavy iron latch, pushed open the door and we stepped down a few steps into the nave. It was

150

dark inside, the air was cool, and there was a musty smell that seeped into the nostrils. Our eyes took a few moments to adjust to the dimness. The interior was an odd mixture of styles: the dun-coloured stone was painted with classical designs on the back wall, brightly coloured murals were on the side wall, and in the side chapels painted statues of saints were perched on high ledges. Half hidden in a corner was an ancient baptismal font, a lump of stone with primitive figures of saints carved into the base, so worn they appeared as ghost-like faces emerging from the masonry.

Near the church stood the village war memorial. We looked at the list of names and saw two Cazàgnacs.

The *Mairie* was the only modern building in Péguilhan. The main doors were open; the cleaning lady was polishing the floor. We asked her if it was OK for us to have a look around.

'Of course, be my guest, Mademoiselle, Monsieur,' she said, pleased to play an almost official role.

The main hall was largely empty apart from stacks of chairs along the sides. On the end wall hung a tricolour and below it stood a bust of Marianne, moulded in cream-coloured plaster, the female personification of the Republic wearing a cap of liberty with flying ribbons. Marianne looked rather lonely in the empty hall.

An official notice of the *Fédération de la Chasse* displayed on the front of the *Mairie* stated the duration of the open hunting season, classified by the type of game. Small native game: partridge, pheasant, rabbit and hare. Big game: wild boar, deer and izard. Migratory birds: turtle dove, ortolan, quail and woodcock. Water fowl: duck and teal. The rules for fishing were less strict. They take their game hunting seriously in Gascony. Fur, feather or fin, in Gascony it's fair game!

All was still and peaceful. Above us house martins darted gracefully, swooping and climbing, then disappearing under the eaves. The only traffic through the centre of the village was the occasional small van coming and going, a tractor hauling a trailer of round hay bales, or one pulling a manure spreader, encrusted with muck around the back end. Van and tractor drivers alike waved to us as they drove by.

A small herd of goats lived in a yard behind a solid wooden fence, beside a house near the centre of the village. We knew the goats were there without even looking over the fence, their natural goat's cheese smell was nose-wrinklingly strong.

In another garden stood a pomegranate tree, studded with bold scarlet flowers. Fruit trees grew well around Péguilhan: peach trees with their elegant leaves and velvety fruit, damson trees raining bloomy purple fruit in August, and fig trees with their shapely leaves. Trees grew by the roadside throughout the village and along the surrounding lanes, the half-wild offspring of orchards and gardens, the fruit was anyone's to gather when it started to fall.

We walked on to the other side of the village, to a road neither of us had ever ventured up before. We passed a big farm with grapevines trained as a hedge around the yard. Rambling, open-fronted barns were used as stores for wood, hay and machinery. The barns stood slowly disintegrating, the wood of the walls weathered to silvery grey, the tiles on the rooves coming loose.

Suddenly we heard a noisy diesel engine start up. Out of the barn drove Monsieur Fustignac on his vintage green tractor. Sitting on the side seat over the wheel arch was Madame Parle-Beaucoup from the café. So the rumours were true! Monsieur Fustignac was wearing his beret and a red-and-white neckerchief. Madame Parle-Beaucoup was wearing her best flower-patterned dress. Her plumpness spilled over the sides of the small seat. Despite their age, they seemed like a couple of teenagers out on a joyride.

An old tractor was a common sight beside many of the houses in Péguilhan. Even if the tractor didn't run any more, it showed the owner's agricultural credentials. Jacques-Henri's old Renault tractor was a good example. Monsieur Fustignac's was the best we'd seen, the oldest and the shiniest – and it still worked. The single-cylinder engine throbbed heavily. Sticking up vertically at the front beside the engine was a tall exhaust tower, with a bulbous, onion-shaped top that vibrated and spluttered puffs of smoke. Fustignac did a few reckless circuits of the farmyard, sending chickens clucking and scattering. The make of the tractor was Percheron, with a stylised red Percheron draught horse moulded into the front. The horse design was very appropriate. As the prancing black stallion on a Ferrari badge expresses the speed and temperamental nature of the Italian sports car, so the sturdy Percheron horse expresses the solid pulling power of the old tractor. In Péguilhan, driving a vintage green Percheron tractor was like cruising in a classic red Ferrari Gran Turismo. Only slower. It obviously did the trick for old Fustignac.

The luvved-up couple gave us the thumbs-up as they came our way. Before they got themselves too over-excited, Monsieur Fustignac drove the tractor back into the barn, stopped the engine and helped Madame Parle-

Beaucoup down from her perch. Giggling between themselves they disappeared from sight, leaving us with mental pictures we would have preferred not to have.

# LES-GENS-DU-CHÂTEAU

THE MAIN ROAD THROUGH PÉGUILHAN SWERVED TO GO ROUND the crumbling, moss-covered wall that encircled the grounds of the château. Set behind massive iron gates, the château stood almost in the centre of the village, but defiantly apart from it. It was a private home and the gates were nearly always locked. The building stood on an elevated terrace. It had a forbidding, unwelcoming appearance. The front was long and flat, with repetitive rows of green wooden-shuttered windows along each storey; the shutters were mostly closed. It was the biggest building in Péguilhan, although everything is relative: it was a very small village, and this was more a *manoir* than a full-sized château.

The owners were still spoken of by the villagers in Péguilhan with a sense of feudal reverence as *les Gens du Château*, the people from the château, the folks at the big house. The phrase was said as if it was all one word, *les-gens-du-château*. The owners were away for most of the year and only descended on the village occasionally. They were quite distinct from people in the village. There were *les-gens-du-château* and *les-gens-du-coin* or, as they said in the local accent, *les-gens-du-cwaing*.

When they returned in July, Monsieur and Madame from the château phoned to book a table for dinner in the restaurant.

'*Les-gens-du-château*, they're coming to dine at the Auberge!' said Jacques-Henri, as he put down the phone.

155

This was a coup. It was more important than ever to create a good impression. *Les-gens-du-château* had booked a few days ahead and asked for something typical. Jacques-Henri and Marie-Jeanne had a long, animated discussion about what to prepare, and in the end they decided on *daube d'oie*, casseroled goose, a rich and hearty peasant stew.

The dish took a day and a half to prepare. Generous pieces of goose were marinated in a whole bottle of red Madiran wine, flavoured with herbs, bay leaves, cloves and seasoning. After marinating them overnight, Marie-Jeanne fried the goose pieces in goose fat, along with onions, carrots and celery. She poured the marinade back over the meat and left the *daube* to simmer for about three hours in a big *marmite*, adding a *bouquet garni* of fresh herbs tied with string. As the slow-cooking *daube* bubbled gently in the pot, the lid rattled quietly from time to time, as if to let us know that all was well. The kitchen was filled with the most enticing smell, which drifted into every corner of the building.

'*Ça donne de l'appétit!*' Marie-Jeanne remarked, noticing me sniffing the aroma.

While the *daube* was simmering, Marie-Jeanne made a *croustade aux pommes* for dessert, with a good splash of Armagnac on top and *crème anglaise* to go with it.

Jacques-Henri wrote out by hand two copies of a souvenir menu, one for Madame, one for Monsieur. Using an old-fashioned black-and-gold fountain pen, his strong farmer's hand produced surprisingly neat handwriting. He signed both copies of the menu with *lou paisan gascoun*. By signing himself the Gascon peasant, Jacques-Henri wasn't putting himself down, he was showing how he belonged there, how his place in the village was as certain as that of the people from the château. Besides, he hoped they'd tell their friends about the excellent food. It could only be good for business.

Marie-Jeanne was in the kitchen giving orders.

'Can you prepare those vegetables?' she said to Florence.

'Can you rearrange the tables to make more space?' she said to Paul.

'And now can you lay the tables?' she said to Anja.

'*Pattes – dehors!*' she ordered Pattes.

At about half past seven, everything was ready.

*Les-gens-du-château* drove the short distance through the village from the château to the Auberge in their Range Rover, *la Range*. It was important to have the right transport.

Jacques-Henri and Marie-Jeanne greeted them at the front door, shaking hands very cordially, and showed them to their table by the front window.

Monsieur was tall, with an aquiline nose and an aristocratic mien. He was dressed carefully casually in an Argyle-pattern sweater. Madame had long dark hair tied back in a neat French plait. She was dressed more smartly in a slightly old-fashioned charcoal-grey New Look dress. It was hard to tell how old they were. Their impassive expressions gave little away.

All the proper formalities were observed; well, as formal as formalities ever were at the Auberge.

'*Madame, Monsieur, asseyez-vous,*' said Jacques-Henri, pulling out their chairs.

As soon as they were seated, he presented them with their handwritten menus.

First, an aperitif. The classic Gascon aperitif is *floc de Gascogne*, a blend of Armagnac and grape juice. *Floc* means bouquet of flowers in Gascon. At the Auberge some things tended to be improvised. Jacques-Henri made a home-made version of the drink. He uncorked a bottle of grape juice, poured out a glassful, carefully poured in a glass of Armagnac, then pushed the cork back in, gave the bottle a swirl and served the aperitif.

It accompanied the starter of whole *foie gras*, with puréed apricots and fingers of bread. A composition for refined palates.

'I would like to propose for you a very good Madiran wine,' Jacques-Henri suggested, pronouncing Madiran as *Madiraing*, and showing them a bottle of Madiran Château Vézac. Monsieur graciously accepted the proposal.

Marie-Jeanne and Anja brought out the main course of *daube* in a big serving dish. As Marie-Jeanne lifted the lid of the pot, meaty nuggets of goose trembled ever so slightly in the still-simmering stew. Dinner was served.

*'Je vous souhaite un très bon appétit,'* Jacques-Henri said respectfully, stressing the word *très*.

Monsieur and Madame from the château took their time over their meal. Jacques-Henri talked with us in the kitchen. He'd had a few slugs of Armagnac by then; after all, the bottle was open...

Jacques-Henri was a wily peasant. He saw through the rituals associated with food and the play-acting of eating out in restaurants. He said that restaurants as we know them are a modern idea, so everyone can afford to go out sometimes, to be waited on and play the role of the *petit-marquis*. In a funny way, he observed, Monsieur and

Madame were doing the opposite, stepping out of the château to enjoy peasant fare at the inn.

When they'd finished their meal, *les-gens-du-château* retired to the terrace outside for a *petite pause* and a relaxing Armagnac *digestif*. In the end they showed themselves to be quite unassuming. They asked questions about the food, and seemed pleased that the restaurant was open and doing well, right on their doorstep. I think the experience was something of a novelty for them: it was the first time they'd been able to eat out in Péguilhan. *Les-gens-du-château* went home impressed. The evening had gone well. Jacques-Henri and Marie-Jeanne were pleased with themselves. The meal was perfectly composed: *foie gras* as a mark of respect for their status and *daube* for a taste of true peasant fare.

*Foie gras* is as essential to Gascony as the haricot and the beret. You can join the debate over which birds produce the finer *foie gras*, ducks or geese, but in Gascony there is no debate over whether or not it has a place on the table.

# VALLEY OF THE LIZARDS

PÉGUILHAN HAD NO POST OFFICE OR POST BOX. THE POSTMAN came to the Auberge every morning in his yellow van, giving a quick beep-beep on his horn to let us know he was there. He delivered the letters, collected the mail to be sent and sold the stamps, all without getting out of his seat.

My twenty-third birthday was in August. The postman delivered some cards sent from England a few days before. 'It looks like someone's having a birthday soon,' he said.

Marie-Jeanne prepared a surprise birthday lunch for me. We had gigot of lamb, cooked in white wine and garlic. The lamb was tender and flaky, it fell away from the bone and almost melted in the mouth. I'd learnt to appreciate the fine meat on the bone. The white wine sauce was delicious, with a strong but subtle flavour.

When we'd nearly finished and only the sauce was left in our plates, Jacques-Henri announced, 'Right, time to *faire chabrot*!'

Literally, *faire chabrot* means 'to do the goat'. Jacques-Henri poured some wine from his glass into the sauce on his plate, gave it a broad swirl, then raised his plate to his lips and drank the thinned sauce from the edge of the plate. We all followed suit. Doing the goat rounded off the course with a great feeling of satisfaction.

Marie-Jeanne baked a birthday cake for me. Because I was English, she made a Victoria sponge. She'd looked up the recipe in a book. This type of cake was well outside her usual repertoire. She added a layer of her own plum jam in the middle and spread white icing on top, finished off with a small red, white and blue striped candle. The cake was a thoughtful gesture and quite touching. I blew out the candle and everyone sang *Joyeux anniversaire*. I felt a little self-conscious at being the centre of attention.

I was given the afternoon off work. Sometimes it was difficult to know what to do with free time in a village so far from anywhere.

Jacques-Henri said casually, '*C'est ton anniversaire, il faut en profiter!*' It's your birthday, make the most of it.

I asked if Anja could also have the afternoon off and Jacques-Henri agreed. We decided to go off and do something touristy. We went to see the ruins of the Roman villa at Montmaurin, in the valley of the river Save, a few kilometres to the south of Boulogne-sur-Gesse.

Standing *en couple* by the roadside looking foreign we found it easy to hitch lifts, first from Péguilhan to Boulogne-sur-Gesse, then to Blajan and on to Montmaurin.

Montmaurin stood on a hill. From the edge of the village we could see the remains of the Roman villa down on the broad, flat valley floor. The ruins were vast, in the shape of an arrowhead, surrounded by trees amid open fields. It was a long walk down to the villa. The valley was completely uninhabited, the air was still and quiet, the only sounds were the faint babble of the river Save, the distant low-pitched hum of a tractor working a field, and the chatter of the crickets that jumped in the long grass wherever we walked.

At the entrance to the villa we paid the twenty franc admission fee to the *guardienne*, who sat in a small office set against the back wall of the ruins. We were the only visitors that afternoon and she kindly offered to come outside and give us a personal tour of the ruins.

We stood in one corner of the villa, by the remains of a low stone wall.

'The villa dates back to the first century AD,' the *guardienne* told us. 'It was the home of a wealthy Gallo-Roman and his family. He chose this site here in this sheltered valley because it was such fertile farming land and there was a constant supply of cool water from the River Save, which you can hear...'

She stopped for us to listen.

'The villa grew into a sprawling complex,' she continued, 'with about a hundred and fifty rooms. It was like a self-contained small town, with private apartments, terraces, gardens, kitchens, a gymnasium and a temple.'

We walked around the edge of a colonnaded bath. Now shaded by an oak tree, it looked like a cool refuge from the afternoon heat.

'This was the thermal wing. It contained a sequence of cold, warm and hot baths, which the Romans loved. *C'était le bon vivre de l'époque*, the good living of the age. The height of indulgence was the icehouse, under there,' she pointed, 'for storing fresh shellfish, brought all the way from the Atlantic and the Mediterranean.'

'What type of shellfish?' asked Anja, curious.

'They've found oyster, mussel, scallop and clam shells,' the *guardienne* explained. 'Life in the villa was good for about a hundred and fifty years, until it was destroyed by a flood. It was rebuilt, then about a hundred years later it was destroyed again, this time by fire. After this second catastrophe, it was abandoned for ever.'

The whole place was alive with small, slim grey-brown lizards. Some were tiny; some of the bigger ones were as long as my hand. Undisturbed, they lay spread-eagled on the walls, clinging on with their dainty feet, warming their bodies in the hot sun. At our approach they scurried in all directions so quickly we could barely see them, darting like streaks of quicksilver in and out of the ruined walls, around the columns and across the mosaic floor. When they stood still again, the dull patterns of markings on their backs looked like miniature mosaics.

I remarked to the *guardienne* about the number of lizards running everywhere in the ruins.

'It's their home now,' she replied, casually.

The villa at Montmaurin suffered the same fate as many great Roman villas in Gascony following the collapse of the Empire. With attacks by the Visigoths, the Moors and the Vikings, the pleasant setting in the valley by the river was no longer safe, and the villagers retreated to the nearby hilltop where the present-day village of Montmaurin stands. They would have recycled much of the stone from the villa for building materials. The remains of other villas probably lie still undiscovered across Gascony.

# MARKET DAY

I N GASCONY DURING THE THIRTEENTH CENTURY, UNDER English administration, about two hundred *bastides* were built across the countryside. These mediaeval fortified 'new towns' were constructed to foster trade and encourage population growth. Most were built on hilltops for safety. *Bastide* comes from the Gascon word *bastida*, meaning bastion or fortress. They were mainly very small, more like walled villages than walled towns. The founding of a new *bastide* was advertised far and wide, with criers travelling across the country announcing the real-estate opportunities on offer.

Vast tracts of land in southwest France were uncultivated or swathed in forests and the *bastides* brought life and prosperity to the countryside. People came from other parts of France, from England and elsewhere in Europe, for the promise of a better life in new surroundings. The settlers, known as *voisins*, built the town walls and the communal buildings. In return for their labour and skills, each was given their own building plot. These plots were all the same size, to ensure equality among the townspeople from the outset. There was an agreed schedule for completion: the first storey was to be built within the first year, the second within the following year, and the third storey when they were able. Each building was slightly different, according to the individual needs and taste of its owner, although all were variations on the same idea.

Some bastides were square, some linear and others radial. The plan was adapted to suit the local terrain, but all had a central rectangular market square lined with stone arcades, supporting beamed ceilings, a feature known locally as *cornières* or *garlanda*. In the centre of the square stood a covered market hall, where sheep, cattle and other goods could be sold under cover.

Traders of every description set up shop under the arches, selling animals, food, salt, wine, pottery and cloth. The arcaded squares were the purpose-built shopping centres of their time and on market days they would have been crowded, noisy, smelly places, full of people, geese, ducks, pigs, goats and any other animals that were for sale. Along the side streets were artisanal workshops, usually run by a master craftsman helped by one or two *compagnons*, apprentices or journeymen, who lived with their master on a more or less equal footing. In the *bastides* of the Comminges, with so many sheep on the hills, there was plenty of work for spinners and weavers. Local consuls checked on the products being made – mediaeval quality control!

Gascony enjoyed strong traditions of freedom and equality, which were reflected in life in the *bastides*. *Voisins* had many privileges, and all had a say in the running of the town. They were allowed to hunt, fish and farm the surrounding countryside and to arm themselves to defend their *bastide* against attack.

It was a land of local *seigneurs* rather than great over-lords. Each *bastide* was closely tied to one manor or abbey. The *bastide* of Boulogne-sur-Gesse was founded in 1283 by the Abbé Taillefer, Superior at the nearby Abbey of Nizors. It was built on a grid pattern with a central square and four main streets, each leading to a town gate. It was named after Bologna in Italy, chosen because Abbé Taillefer had been a student there.

The modern-day Boulogne-sur-Gesse was the nearest town to Péguilhan and provided all the necessary shops and services: the *gendarmerie*, the *Maison d'agriculture*, a *lycée*, banks, clothes shops, food shops including two *boulangeries*, two pharmacies and the local abattoir.

Wednesday was market day. It was the high point of the week for many locals. Notices on the arches forbade parking in the square and the town centre was closed to traffic.

Anja and I went to the market one Wednesday near the beginning of August. The square was full of stalls under striped awnings, selling clothes and household goods. Food stalls were confined to the edges and the side streets. All the basic necessities of domestic life were available: brushes, mops, buckets and cleaning products, ornaments, knickknacks, bags and all sorts of everyday items. The market goers were mostly older people. Stout, middle-aged women, carrying chequer-patterned shopping bags, carefully examined the wares on each stall. Old men wearing berets sat on white plastic chairs in the shade under the arches in front of the grandly named Café Bar Hôtel du Parc, chatting and watching people go by. A sense of expectancy hung in the air, as if something exciting was going to happen, even though it was probably exactly the same each week.

Anja and I walked slowly round the square. We felt like two children on a day out, holding hands so we wouldn't lose each other. The market had an endearing simplicity. Although it was old-fashioned, it suited the steady, traditional lives of the Boulonnais, and certainly showed the more idiosyncratic side of Gascon life.

The clothes stalls sold everything to achieve the Boulogne-sur-Gesse 'look'. A womenswear stall displayed full-length, sleeveless, cover-all pinafores in stiff cotton, heavily patterned with flowers on a blue background.

No fewer than three stalls were piled high with women's underwear, offering mountains of knickers and bras for sale. All ages, sizes, shapes, tastes and occasions were catered for, in every possible colour. The range went from lacy thongs to seriously big pants, made from thick cotton with elasticated waists and knees for older women of ample proportions. Some of the bras were very odd in shape and looked like pairs of white pudding basins. We laughed at this cheeky glimpse into the lives of the female population.

A hat stall sold a variety of headgear in different styles. Hanging up at the front were broad, black Pyrenean berets. Emblazoned in bright red and gold letters inside each beret was the name El Bandido. I couldn't resist trying one on. The stallholder was a tiny man, with a curly Mexican bandit-style mustachio, sporting a wide-brimmed, green tweed hunting hat with a brightly coloured feather in the band. I think he fancied himself a bewhiskered reincarnation of Sancho-the-Terrible. He looked at me with a market trader's eye.

'It suits you,' he said.

'I think it's too small,' I replied.

'No problem,' he assured me. 'I've got berets in all sizes!'

I was about to say that I didn't really want to buy one, I was only looking, when he disappeared into the back of his van to find a beret in my size. He was sure he'd made a sale.

'He's going to make me buy one,' I said to Anja.

'Let's do a runner,' she said. 'Quick, he's not looking.'

No sooner were we out of sight than our noses began to twitch with the strong smell of vinegar. It was coming from a van, where a red-faced, scruffy-looking man, smoking a fat cigar, was selling cheap red wine by the litre from big yellow plastic barrels. The floor was littered with used glass and plastic bottles. Customers could bring their own bottle, or one would be retrieved from the floor. The stall holder opened the tap on the barrel to fill a big blue plastic jug, then poured the wine down a funnel into the customer's bottle. We shuddered to think what it tasted like and what it did to the liver. One customer was eagerly holding out a jug to be filled; he was either going to carry it home or drink the contents on the spot. Poor-quality red wine is the biggest single cause of alcohol-related illness in France; I think we'd identified a culprit.

We walked under the arcade of the market hall, where everything seemed old and worn. The stone columns were pock-marked and gouged in places. In the centre steps led up to the offices of the *Mairie* on the upper storey. We held our noses as we passed the public toilets *à la turque*.

Under the arches, a young woman with long, beaded hair had set up a small stall for a travel company selling Caribbean cruises. She wasn't doing any business.

In a corner, an orange-and-black sign advertised *Tatouage temporaire au Henna*. The woman tattooist, with copper-coloured hair and a long ruffled gypsy skirt, was sitting next to her stall. She raised an eyebrow and smiled welcomingly when she thought she saw a customer approaching, but then quickly looked disappointed.

A very elderly man, with the stature of a garden gnome, stooped and bandy legged, shuffled towards her. He was wearing a broad, floppy beret and a check shirt, the waistband of his grey trousers pulled up to just below his armpits. And on his feet were orange corduroy slippers – just the thing for market day. The tattooist waited patiently until he drew near, agonisingly slowly. When he finally reached her stall, he looked curiously at the orange sign, which matched his slippers. He bent farther forward, with his hands crossed behind his back, to ask her what she did. She explained about temporary henna tattoos, pointing to the designs displayed on a board. The old man raised his hands in a gesture that obviously meant henna tattoos were not for him!

Later on, we saw the same old man causing a hold-up as he backed out of the doorway to the *pharmacie*. This was in the main street off the square and was impossible to miss. Jutting out from the wall above was a neon sign, a green flashing cross, showing the time of day, the temperature and the shop opening times. With gleaming plate-glass windows set in stainless-steel frames, spot-lit window displays and electric sliding doors, it was the most modern shop in Boulogne-sur-Gesse. A trip to the *pharmacie* appeared to be the new religion – no one went into the church opposite, but there was a steady stream of customers in and out of the *pharmacie*. They all left with a carrier bag full of items, well prepared to indulge in the French pastime of over-medicating oneself.

A mature woman came outside and stood on the pavement accompanied by a white-coated assistant. They put their heads together in a conspiratorial way, comparing the benefits of the different products in the white boxes they were holding. This was obviously a problem of a delicate and intimate nature, which could not be discussed in front of other customers.

Then the cyclists made their entrance to the square. There were six of them, three couples, the sort of Brits I dread meeting abroad. Middle-aged and overweight, they had squeezed into bright Lycra cycling outfits and fancied themselves in the Tour de France. They formed their own small *peloton*, about three weeks behind the main race. They pulled up outside the café, leant their bikes against the arches, and took over two tables. The local men eyed them from under their berets and chuckled, but the British cyclists didn't notice. The men all had paunches; the women were rather big-bottomed for their cycling shorts. The purple, orange and pink Lycra, glistening in the sunlight, stretched over their bodies, making them look like a group of assorted balloon sculptures. They ordered *citrons pressés* all round. How very French! Their leader, with a pink face and a ridiculous comb-over that was standing vertical from the effect of cycling, made rude remarks very loudly in English about the French people around them, assuming no one could understand. Anja and I walked away, embarrassed for them.

Two elderly ladies in blue and green pinafore dresses looked disdainfully at the British cyclists. '*Par pitié!*' said one. For pity's sake! The other agreed and they shrugged their square shoulders.

Anja and I turned our attention to the food stalls, selling fresh produce from all over Gascony and across the Spanish border. Most were lorries and vans with drop-down sides, which travelled from market to market over a wide area.

The butcher's stall, *Boucherie – Viandes – Gibiers*, sold all the bits of pigs, cows, sheep and game, and more tripe than we cared to look at. Along its front whole rabbits were hanging up by hooks through the tendons in their back legs. The butcher warned us there was lead shot inside. These had clearly been wild rabbits.

At the poulterer's stall, *La Volaillerie*, plump ducks and geese were lined up in rows, neatly plucked and trussed, ready for the oven.

At the charcuterie stall, *Produits Régionaux*, there was *lapin en gelée*, chunks of rabbit preserved in a terrine of clear jelly. There was also a white oblong dish of *fromage de tête*. We weren't fooled by the name – *fromage de tête* had nothing to do with cheese, it was everything from a pig's head cooked and pressed into a mould. On close inspection, we could just make out bits of tongue and brain squashed together. Taking pride of place in the centre of the charcuterie display was the speciality of Boulogne-sur-Gesse, *terrine de daube à la boulonnaise*, a beef stew cooled and pressed in long terrines, cut by the slice like pâté.

The adjacent stall was a family business specialising in duck and goose products: *Foie Gras – Oie – Canard – Françoise et Denis Gaujacq et leur Fille – Produits de la Ferme*. Everything was sold in tins and preserving jars: *pâté de campagne, jarrets de porc, rillettes de canard à l'ancienne, confit d'oie, terrine de lièvre, terrine de caille, terrine de sanglier*... The phrase 'local speciality' is often a euphemism for something other people wouldn't eat. Monsieur and Madame Gaujacq tried to persuade us to buy a local speciality, *cou farci de canard*, a duck's neck stuffed with *foie gras*, duck meat and figs, in a tubular tin. Er, no thank you.

Our noses led us quite naturally to the cheese stall, *Artisans Fromagers Affineurs*, which seemed a more tempting option. We tried slices of different types. Anja liked the Cabécou creamy goat's cheese and we bought a couple of rounds. Having given us quite a few samples, I think the woman on the stall was a little piqued that we didn't want to buy anything else.

The various fruit and vegetable stalls were a colourful sight. We stopped at *Les Produits du Pays*, which had a green and yellow canopy above huge, misshapen Marmande tomatoes, crisp lettuces, giant courgettes, cucumbers, artichokes, green beans, onions, garlic, stacks of pink and red radishes and a small mountain of *cornichons*. The stallholder was a jolly man in green overalls, who struck up a conversation and cracked a joke with any potential customer.

The fruit stall nearby had a mouth-watering display, wooden trays of full, ripe fruit: peaches, both red and yellow fleshed, large Agen plums, small yellow *mirabelles*, grapes, stacks of yellow melons, and the first apples and pears of the season from Spain. We asked for some delicious-looking apricot-plums. The *fruitière* helpfully told us not to choose our plums from the tray because they were not the best; instead she brought out a fresh tray of even riper and more succulent fruit from under the stall. The apricot-plums had red and orange skin like plums, and the flesh and taste of apricots. They were very juicy: as we bit into them the juice ran through our fingers and dribbled down our fronts.

A stall beside the doors to the church, *Torréfaction Artisanale de Cafés*, sold loose coffee beans and tea from giant round tins, and sweet things like nougat, candied fruit and locally produced honey.

The market was all over by lunchtime, the stalls shut up and driven away. In the afternoon the town went quiet: the square was empty, the streets deserted, the shops closed up and the shutters drawn on the apartment windows above. It seemed that the residents had all gone home for a *sieste* to recover from the excitement. Perhaps they needed to gather their energy for next week.

As I later discovered, we were by no means the first foreigners to pass through this *bastide*. Nearly two hundred years earlier, during the rainy spring of 1814, the Duke of Wellington had garrisoned the British army at Boulogne-sur-Gesse.

Towards the end of the Peninsular War, Wellington invaded southwest France, pursuing the French army under General Soult through southern Gascony. In February, at the battle of Orthez, the Iron Duke was slightly injured when a musket ball hit his sword hilt, bruising his thigh and leaving him limping for several days. The battle-weary army bivouacked at the mediaeval town of Pau to recuperate. Wellington, who never travelled without his hounds, went foxhunting. The rolling countryside of Gascony was ideal for pursuing the local *renard*.

The French withdrew and took the longer but surer route through Saint-Gaudens towards Toulouse. General Soult was a Gascon and he knew the terrain. The British took the shorter route through Boulogne-sur-Gesse and Lombez in an attempt at heading off the French. They had chosen unwisely: the roads through the valleys of the Gesse and the Save were in an awful condition, and they had problems with rain, mud and swollen rivers.

Wellington garrisoned his army of about 50,000 troops at Boulogne-sur-Gesse on 23 March. The arrival of so many soldiers was a serious concern for the local population, and the small town must have been overwhelmed. The Boulonnais need not have feared. Wellington was a strict disciplinarian and issued an order that every scrap of his men's provisions was to be paid for. When a local farmer complained that one of his geese was missing, straight away a search was mounted for the bird. The missing goose couldn't be found, until some soldiers started laughing at the sound of flapping and squawking coming from inside a drummer-soldier's drum. The stolen goose was extracted, given back to the farmer, and the soldier was duly punished.

There was another problem with bullock carts being taken by the army without the owners' consent, for carrying food and equipment. Wellington issued an order that commandeered carts were to be returned to their owners and payments made in full. In future, no bullock cart was to be kept by the army for longer than a day's march.

The local population came to welcome Wellington and his troops as liberators. The French army had not behaved so well: the Duke authorised local mayors to form urban guards, to protect the Gascons from marauding French soldiers.

The presence of the British army at Boulogne-sur-Gesse left no permanent mark, as if the town were simply too small to meet the grand events of history face to face. Wellington and his troops stayed there briefly, then moved on, leaving the town to get on with its business. On 24 March the British reached L'Isle-en-Dodon, where Wellington issued an order that because of the wet weather, all infantry soldiers and non-commissioned officers were to be issued with new shoes, gratis.

Wellington caught up with General Soult at Toulouse in early April. The battle outside the city on 10 April was a decisive victory for the British and ended the military campaign in the southwest. Wellington was received as a conquering hero. The Prefect and the Mayor of the city had fled. The Deputy Mayor and most of the municipal council, with the Urban Guard drawn up in rank, accompanied by a band and a vast assembly of citizens, waited to greet Wellington at one of the main gates to the city. Unfortunately, the Duke didn't know about this, and he entered by another gate. Everyone made a dash to the main square, where the whole delegation hastily reassembled. A messenger ran off to tell Wellington, who was a little confused when he was finally led into the square. Amid great cheers and applause, the Deputy Mayor presented him with the keys to the city on a velvet cushion while the French band played *God Save the King*.

When peace was formally declared, the town hall, known as the Capitole, was decked out with laurel branches and royalist banners. The Toulousains threw Napoleon's statue out of the window; they had had enough of the tyrant and the trouble he had caused. While the Allied generals ate dinner in the Capitole and toasted their victory with champagne, the news reached them of Napoleon's abdication six days earlier at Fontainebleau.

A spin-off from the Gascony campaign was the development of tourism in Pau. Many of the officers in Wellington's army had been so delighted with the town during the bivouac there that at the end of the Napoleonic Wars, some veterans of the campaign returned and began developing the mediaeval town into a Victorian health resort. It quickly grew famous for the healing effects of its rarefied climate and the benefits of the local mineral waters. By the middle of the nineteenth century it was a star resort for the British, a genteel outpost of the Empire. It became known as Pau-Ville-Anglaise, a playground for leisured tourists and expatriates.

In 1856, the British built the first golf course in continental Europe just outside Pau on the Plaine de Billère, a well-drained stretch of land next to the river with a view of the old town gates and the Pyrenees as a backdrop. The course was a full 18-holer, and for the nineteenth hole they built a comfortable bay-windowed clubhouse, to accommodate their collection of portraits and silver trophies. The British in Pau liked their games: they also built a race track, a polo field, a cricket pitch, tennis courts and a casino.

EL BANDIDO

# FESTIVAL WEEK

THE BIGGEST DATE IN THE LOCAL CALENDAR WAS APPROACHING: 15 August, feast day of *la Sainte Marie de l'Assomption*, the patron saint of Boulogne-sur-Gesse, when the town held its annual *fête*, temporarily transforming the old *bastide*. The *fête* went on for a whole week, peaking with a firework display and a *banda* concert. The festivities embraced the entire canton, including Péguilhan, too small to hold its own *fête*.

Posters appeared weeks before in Boulogne-sur-Gesse and in the surrounding villages. We picked up a programme from the *Mairie* in Péguilhan. The list of events was typed out rather unevenly on one side of a sheet of A4 paper; I hope nothing gets lost in translation:

```
     FESTIVALS OF BOULOGNE-SUR-GESSE
  GRAND FESTIVAL OF CARNIVAL ACTIVITIES
     A WARM WELCOME AWAITS YOU

Saturday 11th August
2pm BOULES COMPETITION IN PAIRS at the
    Boulodrome (500 francs + trophies +
    guaranteed fixtures)
4pm GOOSE RACE - BETTING (Place de la
    Mairie)
10pm BALL-DISCO with band: HIGH FREQUENCY

Sunday 12th August
8.30am FISHING COMPETITION AT THE LAKE (200
    francs in prizes)
8.30pm COUNTRY MEAL (50 francs)
```

Monday 13th August
3pm SKITTLES COMPETITION (numerous prizes)
4pm BOULES COMPETITION IN TEAMS OF THREE (1000
    francs + trophies + guaranteed fixtures)

Tuesday 14th August
9.30pm TORCHLIGHT PROCESSION WITH PIPE BAND

Wednesday 15th August
6am FANFARE AWAKENING
10am MASS - Church of Our Lady of the
    Assumption
12 noon GREASY POLE
3pm PROCESSION OF CARNIVAL FLOATS, BANDAS,
    MAJORETTES
7pm BANDA FESTIVAL
9pm SENSATIONAL FIREWORK DISPLAY launched over
    THE LAKE sponsored by LACROIX INDUSTRIES.
    The best pyro-musical display in the Southwest!

Thursday 16th August
3pm CHILDREN'S GAMES
10pm ACCORDION BALL. TREASURES OF THE ACCORDION
    with the orchestra of ALAIN MISICHINI, world
    champion accordionist

Friday 17th August
ALL DAY AT THE TOWN HALL:
EXHIBITION OF OLD POSTCARDS (Canton of Boulogne)
BEARS OF THE PYRENEES and VARIOUS
EXHIBITION OF POSTAGE STAMPS
EXHIBITION OF PAINTING (local painter)
3pm CONCERT AT THE RETIREMENT HOME

        Celebrate and live life to the full!


The goose race on Saturday afternoon was hilarious. The
sight of startled palmipeds running in a confused gaggle
around the town square was definitely the funniest thing
I saw all summer.

In the morning, barriers were set up to mark out the circuit, one complete lap of the Place de la Mairie. At 4 o'clock sharp, the race began. The geese were brought out of a pen and herded towards the starting line. They were wearing stylish red satin sashes like neckerchiefs and numbered collars for identification. The referee called out *Prêts*! *Partez*! and fired his starting pistol. Bang! And they're off! Well, almost. Frightened by the noise, the geese started running, then slowed to a waddle, then began to disperse. They looked at the crowd with indignation; some cackled and one or two even hissed angrily. A couple of geese were having none of it and they started heading back the wrong way. A man came running up, waving a baton with a red sash tied to the end. He managed to encourage all the geese to put on a final spurt for the finish line, where they were rewarded with small heaps of corn.

The owner of the winning goose, a portly, unshaven farmer wearing blue overalls and a beret, rushed in and lovingly picked up his bird. With a beaming grin, he proudly held it aloft for all to see. The startled bird waved its webbed feet in the air; the onlookers cheered, applauded and whistled. I don't know if the goose appreciated being the centre of such noisy attention.

The betting system was quite informal but seemed to be taken seriously, and at the end of the race I noticed small wads of 100 franc notes changing hands discreetly.

The original purpose of goose racing was to tone the muscles in the animals' thighs, which improved the flavour. Nowadays, geese are raced just for sport.

On Wednesday, as the high point of the festival approached, we all drove down to Boulogne-sur-Gesse.

We met a *route barée* – road closed – sign on the approach road and had to park and walk.

The streets were thronged with people, who must have come in from every village, hamlet and farm for many kilometres around. The *festoyeurs* were out to enjoy themselves to the maximum. Whole families had turned out. Some children were wearing fancy dress, while older people disported themselves in their best clothes.

We heard the carnival procession before we saw it. No sooner had we sat down at the last two empty tables in front of the Café Bar Hôtel du Parc than we felt the thump-thump through the ground of the *banda* starting up round the corner of the square. Women dancers led the procession, dressed in long, elaborate white costumes with bright sleeves and rainbow headdresses.

The dancers were followed by the first marching *banda*, Los Novillos Banda, the resident *banda* of Boulogne-sur-Gesse, belting out a homage to the Gypsy Kings on brass and percussion. Their name was painted in bright red letters on their instruments. The musicians, both men and women, were dressed in white shirts, black trousers, red bandannas around their necks and straw hats. The drums thumped – the heaviest were pushed along on a trolley – the trumpets and trombones hooted, the cymbals crashed, the tuba boomed from over the shoulder of a big man at the back, and every now and then a man with a circular hunting horn gave a good long blast to keep the noise level up.

The carnival had a Spanish feel about it. The local festivals in Gascony are run by Spanish gypsies and by the descendants of Republicans who fled across the border after their defeat in the Spanish Civil War, fought for the

French Resistance during the German Occupation, and remained in Gascony after the war.

The first float came round the corner, representing *Les Trois Mousquetaires*. One of the *mousquetaires* waved his sword threateningly at the onlookers, then put it back in its scabbard and doffed his plumed hat, as if to make peace with everyone again. The float was pulled by an old orange tractor, driven by a man with a bushy moustache, an over-large floppy beret and round glasses. He looked like a comedy Gascon farmer, as the French say *sorti d'un livre*, straight out of a story book.

The next float was a giant goose, about five metres tall, lolling precariously as it moved around the square. The giant figure wore a bright red sash around its neck, and goslings and eggs were arranged at its feet. The thousands of feathers on the geese were made of crêpe paper, so realistic the work must have taken hundreds of hours. Children dressed as peasants sat on the front of the float, wearing hats too big for them, looking as if they were wondering how they got there.

A small boy carrying a purple-and-white banner led the Boulogne majorettes, dressed in purple-and-white uniforms, marching more or less in time as they twirled their batons. A car drove behind them with loudspeakers fixed to the roof blaring out festival music.

The procession of *bandas* continued, each with its own distinctive costume. The floats rolled by, each with a different theme. A group of middle-aged men in drag marched past, dressed as majorettes. They were rustic farmer types with lived-in faces, and looked ridiculous in their blue-and-white costumes with glitter wigs and frilly bloomers. They sang in unison, '*Olé, olé, olé, olé...*'

Tall, upright figures of bulls, about five metres high, walked through the carnival on their hind legs. They were resplendent in toreador costumes of shining blue-and-crimson velvet, decorated with glittering gold braid. The men inside the giant puppets peeped through holes in the bulls' bellies and operated levers to move the long, dangling front legs. Their height was intimidating, but they leant down to pat children's heads with their big front hooves.

The carnival queen was on the last float of the procession. She was poised elegantly inside a magnificent open seashell. The shell was a work of art, covered in brightly coloured crêpe paper in white, yellow, gold and sea green. The queen wore a shiny turquoise sequined dress, shimmering in the sunlight, and a white sash bearing her name, La Belle Jeanneton. At her feet were sheaves of wheat and giant gold coins. The link between the seashell, the wheat and the coins wasn't obvious until the crier on the front of the float called out to the crowd: 'Look at La Belle Jeanneton: she is a hundred times more beautiful than the day is long. Look at La Belle Jeanneton: when she brushes her hair, golden wheat falls from her locks in bushels. Look at La Belle Jeanneton: when she washes her hands, golden Spanish pieces of eight fall from her fingers by the dozen. Look at La Belle Jeanneton: so beautiful she was held prisoner in golden chains by the monster of the deep, until a prince came to rescue her.' La Belle Jeanneton smiled a fixed smile and waved a white-gloved hand, failing to perform any miracles, as the float moved steadily around the square. What very Gascon measures of beauty: wheat and money!

The people on the floats threw handfuls of confetti over the crowd. On one, a man wielded a confetti bazooka.

He was wearing wraparound dark glasses to look mean, but was really enjoying himself. He stuffed handfuls of confetti into the long steel tube, packed it down with a ramrod, took aim and fired an explosive cloud over the onlookers. I took a direct hit from the bazooka: the confetti went down inside my T-shirt and fell out of my shorts. Children came around selling bags of confetti to throw back at the floats; you could take your pick from a blue, pink or green mix.

The noises of the different *bandas*, the music from the loudspeakers, the rumble of the tractor engines, and the shouts and cheers of the crowd drowned each other out in a deafening din that filled the square.

Just when we thought the carnival had finished, the first dancers came round the corner again and the whole procession made a second lap of the town. The comedy farmer with the over-large beret was carrying a beer when he appeared on the second lap. He raised his glass to the onlookers and took a gulp, leaving froth on his moustache.

Two laps were not enough: the procession made four circuits of the town before splitting into breakaway groups and returning to the cover of the *Salle Polyvalente*. The participants had spent so many, many hours making their costumes and floats, they wanted to be sure everyone got a good look. If the procession had done a few more laps of the town I don't think anyone would have minded, everyone was in such high spirits. By the time the procession had finished the town was carpeted with confetti.

The food stalls round the outside of the square and along the side streets sold savoury and sweet festival foods. They were painted in garish colours: flamingo pink, peacock blue, canary yellow and acid green.

The menu at the savoury food stall *La Croquandise* was classic southwest fare: *frîtes, frîtes-magret, merguez, brochette, ventrèche* and *jambon-épaule*. The sweet stall was called *Le Festival du Sucre*. It sold real fairground food: *barbe à papa, pommes d'amour, churros, chi chi, beignets, gaufres* and *glaces*. We tried some *churros*, long curly fingers of piped waffle batter, fried in front of us, dipped in sugar and served in a cornet, about a dozen at a time.

The drinks tent, *La Bodéga*, was doing a fast trade in *jacqueline*, a local punch made with white wine, grenadine syrup and lemonade. It was cheap, at five francs a go, and was ladled out into plastic glasses, with chunks of fruit floating on top.

In the shooting gallery, *Tir aux Canards*, tin ducks moved on a conveyor belt in front of the back wall painted with a lake scene. A sign promised a win at every turn, *à tous les coups on gagne*, so I decided to have a go. I hit some ducks, winning a small orange furry toy that neither Anja nor I particularly wanted, so we gave it to a nearby child.

The children's version of the shooting gallery, *Pêche aux Canards*, was a fishing game, where small plastic ducks bobbed along a moving stream of water and children had to pick them out with miniature fishing rods to win a prize. In Gascony, ducks – real, tin or plastic – didn't stand a chance!

Lucky-dip machines offered punters the chance to swivel the handles of the small crane to grab prizes from inside the big glass boxes. In one box the prizes were all soft toys. In the other they were all women's knickers. Knickers as prizes in a fairground lucky dip? It just didn't seem right. If a man succeeded in grabbing a pair, did he give them to his sweetheart? *Here you are darling – some nice pants I won for you at the fairground*! And if a woman won them, supposing she grabbed the wrong colour or the wrong size, could she ask to exchange them? Best not to speculate, we thought.

Traditional fairground rides were set up in the open square in front of the post office: waltzers, dodgems and a small carousel for children, *La Féerie Enfantine*, painted in the brightest colours and covered with flashing bulbs.

As dusk approached the lights of the town came on. Boulogne-sur-Gesse had put on the full display of a Gascon town *en fête*. Illuminated stars, crescent moons and comets hung on wires suspended between the buildings. Garlands of coloured lanterns were draped across the square, twinkling in the darkness.

Beneath the arches of the market hall, the *bandas* tuned up to perform a concert, each in turn. The musicians swayed in time to the cheerful rhythm of their instruments. The *bandas* had a real oompah-oompah sound. Gascon castanets, known as *tricanetas*, added a Spanish accent to the music. The *bandas* played some favourite and familiar tunes: *La Bamba, Faire la Fête, Viva la Fiesta, La Macarena, La Cucaracha...*

In front of the musicians, revellers danced. Women and girls twirled in time to the music, wearing scarlet and yellow flowers coquettishly placed in their glossy black hair. Eager young men danced energetically, jutting out their elbows and lifting their feet. Older men did a soft-shoe shuffle by the sidelines, including the old man with the orange corduroy slippers, which he had kept on for the *fête*. We recognised him by his stoop and his slow movements before we noticed his footwear. Couples took to the floor as the evening went on. The music was infectious, so Anja and

I joined in. We didn't dance in the same way as the locals, but nobody minded. As the evening livened up and the *jacqueline* flowed, men raised their glasses in drunken salutes, women grabbed their skirts as they danced, and finally all the *bandas* played together, working themselves up for a spirited rendition of *When the Saints Come Marching In*.

Shortly before nine o'clock in the evening, the mayor walked importantly down the steps of the *Mairie* from the offices above. *Monsieur le Maire* was in casual wear for the evening, but nonetheless wearing his blue, white and red sash, to distinguish his office. Pausing on the bottom step, he held up his microphone and pushed a button to switch it on. A loudspeaker system was permanently in place on the buildings around the square for the civic authorities to address the people. Puffing out his chest, the mayor announced that it was now time to go down to the lake to see the firework display. He made his proclamation as long-winded as possible.

'*Oyez, oyez, bonnes gens, Mesdames et Messieurs, chers Boulonnais…*'

His voice was distorted as it crackled through the loudspeakers and echoed around the buildings, getting lost in the hubbub of people who were having too much fun to listen to him.

The festival goers made their way down the hill. The lake that the Boulonnais were so proud of was really a very large duck pond. We assembled on the shore, much to the surprise of some nearby ducks who had bedded down for the night. I could see figures with torches moving about in the dark on the opposite side, getting the fireworks ready. There were trees near the bank. *When the fireworks go up*, I thought, *they'll crash straight into the trees*, but this obstacle didn't seem to bother the local pyrotechnicians. We waited for a few minutes, then suddenly loud music started and fireworks shot into the sky. The crowd gasped as one firework after another whooshed and exploded, colours cascading into the night. The reflections in the water added to the drama. Children sat on grownups' shoulders, ooohing and aaahing, clapping their hands with excitement and approval.

When the fireworks were over, people started to make their way back up the hill to the town. Paul and Florence had gone off by themselves. Anja and I walked slowly back. In town, we stood under the arcade to wait for the others. Anja was wearing a long, black linen summer dress, tapered at the waist. An evening chill brushed against us as the raw night air of the countryside drifted in. We warmed ourselves with a slow kiss in the shadow of the arches. Some merry locals shouted words of encouragement, but we took no notice.

Boulogne-sur-Gesse had done itself proud. The festival was honest, good-natured fun. For country people, surrounded day after day by fields and woods and dull sounds, the festival was an exuberant expression of their need to be part of a happy crowd and for spontaneous explosions of colour and noise.

une fedayeuse

187

# LA GUINGUETTE

O N SATURDAY NIGHTS WHEN THERE WAS NO FÊTE WE
went to a nightclub called La Guinguette. It was
basically a shed in a field, named after an old-
fashioned dance hall, part in the open air. To this day I
couldn't say where it was, because we went in the dark,
came back in the dark, and I never did the driving. On our
way, if we were lucky, we managed to tune the car radio
into La Voix d'Armagnac FM, broadcasting *en direct* from
Gabarret, to get us in the party mood.

We normally arrived at La Guinguette at about ten in
the evening. Parked cars lined the lane, so we had to park
some distance away. There was no charge at the door and
the bar sold only bottled beer. Inside, music boomed out
from speakers attached to the roof beams, while clubbers
jiggled about in the cramped room. By the early hours of
the morning the inebriated and the tired stood outside,
sleeping upright against the wooden walls of the building.

The atmosphere at La Guinguette was more like an
extended family party than a nightclub. Most people
knew each other and they came and went all evening,
quite casually. We usually left at about four o'clock in the
morning, by which time the exhaustion of staying up all
night seemed a heavy price to pay. We would drive home
bleary-eyed, with dawn breaking.

I still remember my first Saturday night at La
Guinguette. An electronic dance track, *Bo le lavabo*, was
played over and over again. I recall some of the lyrics:

*Ho, ho, ho, qu'il est beau*
*Qu'il est beau*
*Qu'il est beau, le lavabo,*
*Lavabo, qu'il est beau*
*Il est beau, le lavabo.*
*Hé, hé, hé, qu'il est laid*
*Qu'il est laid, le bidet,*
*Le bidet, il est laid*
*Il est laid, le bidet.*

It makes no more sense in English than it does in French:

Ho, ho, ho, how handsome he is
How handsome he is
How handsome he is, the washbasin,
Washbasin, how handsome he is
He is handsome, the washbasin.
Hey, hey, hey, how ugly he is
How ugly he is, the bidet,
The bidet, he's ugly
He's ugly, the bidet.

Satirical, apparently.

On the journey home, I sat slumped in the back of the car, Anja sideways on my knee, her head against the door pillar. *Bo le lavabo*, repetitive and hypnotic, thumped continuously in my ears. Paul was behind the wheel, he braked sharply and there was a thud on the front of the car. We'd run over a fox. Sprawled by the side of the road, it was clearly dead. There was nothing we could do for it and we drove on. In the fuzziness of half-sleep, I hardly noticed. *Bo le lavabo* just carried on thumping inside my head.

We sometimes saw Hans and Lotte at La Guinguette. They stood out from the locals. Lotte danced intensely, swaying and dipping to the music as if in a trance. Whenever I spoke to her she was very vague, her eyes glazed; I think she was stoned. Anja spoke to her in German and seemed to get more sense out of her than I could. Hans was happy to stand at the bar and talk.

# BETWEEN DOG AND WOLF

ENTRE CHIEN ET LOUP, BETWEEN DOG AND WOLF, IS AN evocative expression, describing that shifting twilight moment that is neither day nor night. One evening at that in-between time, Anja and I met by the swing in the clearing in front of the Auberge.

The air was breathlessly still; we could hear every little sound around us. We whispered so as not to intrude on the stillness. Suddenly, the silence was broken by the sound of desperate whimpering close by. We looked between the trees towards the Auberge, where we saw Pattes cowering against the front door, pleading to be let in. Then we saw the cause of his distress: two wolves came skulking round the corner of the building, followed moments later by two more. In the moonlight we could make out the outlines of their hard, square bodies, with craggy fur and pointed ears. I'd never before seen wolves in the wild. Jacques-Henri had told me about them, but they still came as a surprise.

They seemed to be intimidating Pattes rather than actually threatening him; they were making sure he stayed out of the way of their scavenging. Pattes stared wide-eyed at the prowling wolves, the most terrified dog I'd ever seen.

The family were almost certainly asleep at the farm by now, and we didn't dare let Pattes in through the front door of the Auberge, because there were guests sleeping upstairs. We weren't sure if it was wise to attempt to scare off four wolves by ourselves, so we called to Pattes in hushed voices and he came scampering over. By doing so we made our presence known to the wolves, who stood and glared at us with sullen contempt.

'What do you think we should do?' whispered Anja.

'I think we should stay still and keep quiet,' I said.

Crouching among the trees by the ridge, I could feel Pattes's heart racing as I held him still. Anja and I listened to the sound of his rapid panting, accompanied by the shrill nocturnal chorus of the cicadas and the menacing, padding footsteps of the wolves going back and forth, back and forth. The tension was palpable. We watched the wolves for what seemed like hours, but in reality it probably wasn't very long. Pattes, sitting on his haunches, was torn between wanting to stay close to us for comfort and wanting to flee.

Thankfully, the wolves decided to leave us alone. They sloped off and didn't come back. Pattes was whimpering quietly. We had to give him reassurance before we let him go. After some friendly chest rubbing and a few encouraging words, he trotted off, back to his bed under the stairs in the courtyard.

Anja and I were alone again, enveloped by the musky night-time smell of the vegetation, the contours of the hillside and the clear, starlit air. The night had trembled, then regained its tranquillity. We lay on our backs, Anja with her head in the vee of my shoulder. The stars shone so brightly in the velvet night sky that if we lay still and looked up for long enough, we imagined we could see the movement of the Earth in them.

Perhaps the four wolves had gone back to join the other ninety-six who guard the Golden Flower, *la Flor Daurada*, the magic flower that sings at sunrise with the voice of a nightingale, according to Gascon folklore.

# PLUM PICKING

EVERY GASCON SCHOOLBOY GROWS UP HEARING STORIES OF their national hero D'Artagnan, the embodiment of the spirit of Gascony, the impoverished aristocrat forced to leave his homeland to seek his fortune in Paris. After leaving his family home at the Château de Castelmore, D'Artagnan was half way to Paris when he suspected that some local men were laughing at him because the old horse he was riding was so exhausted it could hardly lift its tail. Quick to anger, he didn't think twice about picking a fight when he was outnumbered. Feeling that his pride was wounded, he charged at the local men. Their ringleader turned his back. D'Artagnan told him to take his sword in his hand and fight like a man. As their leader turned to face the enraged Gascon, his friends ambushed D'Artagnan from behind. D'Artagnan ended up down in the dirt with his face bloodied, relieved of his dignity and his possessions. His hot-headed Gascon temperament could not recognize the thin line between bravery and foolhardiness.

One day in August, Paul and I went to pick plums from the orchard. The hot summer had caused many of them to ripen early. We took a stepladder, two buckets and a rake for pulling down the branches. Paul was carrying two long sticks and he gave one to me.

'*En garde*!' he said, raising his stick like a sword. 'We have to arm ourselves.'

'Why?'

'Plum picking can be dangerous,' he warned.

I imagined we might hurt ourselves falling off the ladder or poke one another in the eye with a branch, but I didn't know why we were taking a soldierly approach to plum picking or who or what we were going to fight.

'*Frelons!*' explained Paul.

The feared creatures known as *frelons* are giant hornets. They can reach four or five centimetres long, they have powerful stings and they're extremely aggressive. They attack in swarms, very angrily when provoked. Paul told me that ten stings can kill a child and twenty can kill an adult. Naturally, *frelons* love plums, which is why they tend to congregate in plum trees and will ambush any unsuspecting pickers who disturb them.

We walked around several trees to choose the ripest fruit. It seemed as though it was going to be a good harvest that year: some plums were purple and ripe, and many more would soon be ripening. We chose a likely-looking tree and stood on either side of it. First, we had to check for *frelons*.

'*Allez!*' Paul cried, and stabbed at the branches with his stick.

*Is this wise?* I thought. I pushed my stick into the branches on my side, moved it about in the foliage, then watched the tree carefully.

'I can't see any over here,' I said.

'Nor me here,' said Paul.

He prodded the tree again with his stick, this time bashing it from side to side between the branches to make a noise. He peered at it intently with his head on one side, half crouching in anticipation, waiting to see if there were any *frelons* lurking among the leaves.

There was a tense moment. '*Frelons*! *Frelons*!' he shouted.

We heard an angry, low-pitched buzzing sound as hornets began to appear threateningly from beneath the leaves.

We both ran away from the tree, bending forward like soldiers taking cover under fire. We stopped at what we judged was a safe distance.

'Well, what do we do now?' I asked.

'Give them time to calm down.'

We waited for a short while, then walked back to the tree we'd just run away from.

'*Un pour tous et tous pour un*!' Paul shouted. One for all and all for one! He seemed to want to pick a fight with the *frelons*. He attacked the tree again, with his feet apart and his left arm raised in the stance of a musketeer. If Paul was D'Artagnan, which musketeer was I? Athos? Porthos? Aramis? The English musketeer?

Paul stood still and looked up into the branches.

'Shouldn't we try a different tree?' I suggested, slightly apprehensive.

'No, it looks fine now.'

'Are you sure?'

'Yeah.'

'Really sure?'

'Of course, let's pick some plums.'

Paul grabbed a branch and pulled it down to reach the fruit. At that moment, dozens of the fearsome insects appeared again, furious at being so rudely disturbed for a second time.

Paul let the branch thwack up into the tree, which made the *frelons* even angrier. We ran away again, but this time some of the *frelons* caught up with us. I got three stings on my forearms. Fortunately, I pinched out two of them before they really started to hurt. I couldn't get the third sting out and could see it pulsating gently under my skin. The area around it turned red and swelled up almost immediately.

'*Aïe! Aïe!*' I heard Paul cry out.

I turned round. He was waving his arms about over his head. He'd been stung on the back of his neck.

Once the *frelons* had settled down, we continued harvesting the plums, both of us still grimacing with the violent, throbbing pain of the stings, hardly speaking a word to each other.

As D'Artagnan admitted, in his youth he had a tendency to pick fights with people who hadn't insulted him at all. It took a few good thumps to the head to knock some sense into him. Paul admitted that the *frelons* hadn't done anything to us until we provoked them. Perhaps the stings would teach us to be more careful next time.

# THUNDER AND LIGHTNING

O NE AUGUST EVENING, JUST AS IT WAS GETTING DARK, the build-up of heat during the day triggered one of Gascony's legendarily violent late-summer thunderstorms.

'*Ça déclenche*,' observed Jacques-Henri ominously, as the thunderstorm rumbled, then let loose its pent-up energy farther down the valley. From the front windows of the Auberge we could see the storm moving towards us.

'*Lou pericle que peta*,' the thunder is roaring, he added in Gascon, recalling the words of his mother tongue. The thunderstorms had etched themselves into the remembered landscapes of his childhood, as dramatic moments when nature was threatening and unkind.

The dogs, Labrit, Mizou, Rôti and Pattes, ran around outside, barking at the noise. As the thunder boomed louder, they became more frightened and ran in. They cowered beneath the table; all except Labrit, who really showed his mettle that evening.

Forked lightning flashed all round, illuminating the landscape with vicious, silvery shafts of light. The air crackled. The lightning backlit the clouds. In front of us towered a monstrous blue-black anvil of a cloud, looking heavier and thicker towards its summit. A thunderbolt struck a tree on a far hilltop and we felt the shockwave. Nature was unleashing its fury. Jacques-Henri uttered a

Gascon saying: '*Susquetot, ne cau pas acessà's devath un àrber!*' Above all, don't take shelter under a tree. He said it as a sort of incantation, as if to protect us from the storm.

Jacques-Henri, Paul and I rushed outside to cover the stack of firewood at the side of the building with a heavy tarpaulin. We got it covered just in time and ran back indoors as the rain started to fall, big drops lashing the leaves and beating the ground.

The electricity cut out, the lights flickering then dying. A power line had been hit. We set up camping torches in the dining room.

Jacques-Henri wanted to go to the farm to check on the animals. He took me and Labrit with him in the Renault. The headlights picked out huge drops of rain in the darkness, falling mercilessly, hitting the car like bullets. Labrit hopped from side to side on the back seat, as anxious as we were. Driving through the storm felt dangerous and exciting.

'It's raining like a pissing cow,' said Jacques-Henri, trying to make light of the situation.

*Some cow!* I thought.

At the farm the cows were huddled together in the bottom corner of the field. The sheep bleated in the *bergerie*, showing the primal fear animals feel about thunder and lightning. Labrit ran around the outside to check that no sheep were loose, getting himself soaked in the process. There was nothing we could do in the dark and the rain, so we drove back to the Auberge.

We all spent the rest of the evening sitting in the dining room, chatting with a few of the guests, waiting for the storm to blow itself out. Jacques-Henri kept everyone entertained by taking his collection of Gascon folktales, by

Jean-François Bladé, down from the shelf and reading several out loud. The stories they told – of ogres in the mountains and fairies in the swamps – seemed ancient and strange. Jacques-Henri knew the tales as if by heart, hardly looking at the book. The thunder was the Bécut, the giant of Gascony, moving rocks about in his cave. If we stayed out of his way he would do us no harm, but anyone who crossed his path would be eaten. While we listened to Jacques-Henri telling us stories of magic and arbitrary cruelty and the storm raged outside, shots of Armagnac all round helped to take the edge off things. At about midnight the Bécut stopped rearranging the rocks in his cave, the sky went quiet and the rain stopped: the storm was over.

In the morning, the power was back on. The engineers from Electricité de France had fixed the problem speedily.

The grass was healthier and greener for a while, but only in patches. The storm had been more electrical than wet and the dark clouds hadn't shed a large volume of water. The ground was so dry that most of the water had run straight off into the rivers and the lake at the bottom of the valley.

'Let's go swimming,' said Paul, the afternoon following the storm. 'The lake will be full.'

The lake was triangular, about a hundred metres across, with woods on two sides. The front shore was flat and muddy, slimy by the water, caked dry at the edges. Small, coarse reeds poked through the mud. Trees overhung the two converging sides of the lake. At the far end, an outcrop of knobbly brown rocks formed a natural promontory over the water.

Paul and Bruno warned me that as well as the fish, we would be sharing the lake with frogs and grass snakes. This information was more off-putting than the muddy bank and the murky water.

'Let's race to the rocks on the other side!' shouted Bruno.

We ran splashing into the water. I'm a good swimmer and I won the race. Bruno was a bit put out by this.

We swam around, taking turns diving from the rocks, splashing and shouting. I love being in water. I took a deep breath and dived towards the bottom, flicking my feet on the surface like a dolphin's tail. A couple of metres down the water was green and much cooler than above. I rolled over, looking up towards the surface, I could see the sun glinting through the trees, greenish-yellow light flickering between rippling shadows.

Our splashing and shouting had disturbed the creatures lurking in the depths. I felt something smooth and lithe brush against my side, touching the soft skin just below my armpit. I flinched. Then something else touched my leg. I swam to the surface. I saw a grass snake swim deftly in front of my face then disappear. Another came over my shoulder and darted away, with its head just out of the water, leaving a wiggly wake behind it. It sent a shiver down my spine and I decided I would really rather not swim with snakes, thank you, so I swam back to the shore and got out of the water. Paul and Bruno weren't bothered and carried on swimming.

Looking into the woods, I noticed what appeared to be ruins some way off among the trees. I was curious and went to investigate. It was shady in the woods beneath the tree canopy. Here and there, narrow shafts of sunlight shone down through the gaps. I picked my way through the undergrowth. The ground was uneven and difficult to walk on, the dry vegetation crackling beneath my feet. Pushing aside some low branches, I stepped out into the small clearing where the ruins lay, apparently the remains of two or three cottages. It wasn't easy to tell how many: all that was left were a few heaps of rubble and some rotting wooden beams. One stone chimneystack was still standing. The place was eerie. Flies buzzed around me. A bird, startled by my presence, flew hurriedly across the clearing and disappeared among the trees, and I heard its wings flap against the leaves.

Feeling uneasy, I went back to join Paul and Bruno, who were out of the water by now. When I asked them about the ruins, Paul said he didn't know much but his father would surely be able to tell me.

Jacques-Henri was only too pleased to be asked and willingly took on the role of storyteller and local historian.

'Those ruined cottages,' he explained, 'once belonged to families of Cagots. Long before I was born, you understand. The Cagots are part of the lore of the region. For centuries they lived scattered throughout Gascony; some also lived over the border in the Navarre in Spain. They were a tribe of outcasts, and to tell you the truth, people here weren't very nice to them. The Cagots were the objects of prejudice and superstition. They were forced to exist on the margins of society. They lived a settled life, they didn't move around like gypsies. No one knows where they came from…'

Jacques-Henri shrugged his shoulders mysteriously.

'Legend has it they were the descendants of lepers,' he continued. 'In those days people believed that leprosy was hereditary and highly contagious. They had a terrible fear of the disease. The Cagots became a caste of untouchables. They were forbidden to walk barefoot in public places, as poor people often did then, and they even had a separate drinking water fountain. Every town had its Cagot quarter, a sort of ghetto known as *la Cagotérie*. Near smaller villages the Cagots lived in isolated hamlets, often in the woods. It was thought that wood did not transmit disease, and so the Cagots were constrained to work with wood, as cutters, joiners, carpenters and carvers. They were made to wear a goose's foot pinned to their tunics to mark them out.'

'Why a goose's foot?' I asked.

'Because people said the Cagots had webbed feet,' he replied, 'and so the goose's foot was a warning.'

'No humiliation was spared them?' I suggested.

'In some towns they had to signal their approach by shaking a rattle,' Jacques-Henri went on. 'Churches usually had a separate side door for the Cagots, known as *la porte des maudits*, the door of the cursed ones. It was low, forcing them to stoop as they went in. Entering through the same door as the Cagots was considered bad luck, so running through the Cagot door was just the sort of stunt children would do for a dare. Once inside the church, the Cagots had to sit at the back, where they had their own holy water font, also marked with a goose foot. The law stated that they could marry only among themselves, *cagot* and *cagotte*. They had no family names, only their given name followed by their collective name, Cagot. They were baptised after nightfall.

'Country people believed that just touching a Cagot could burn your skin. When people travelled to a village they didn't know, an easy way to recognize the Cagots was to look for their earlobes – anyone without earlobes, or with lobes joining the cheek, was quite likely to be a Cagot.'

Jacques-Henri pointed to his own earlobes. 'You see, I've got mine,' he said.

I laughed and agreed that with earlobes like that, he was definitely not a Cagot.

'There are no more Cagots,' he concluded. 'With the Revolution, everyone became a citizen. Those cottages you saw in the woods have been in ruins for as long as I can remember.'

This was all Jacques-Henri could tell me. The origins of the Cagots are a mystery. They were sometimes referred to as *Crestias*, Christians, possibly because lepers were known in mediaeval times as *pauperes Christi*. Leprosy is only one explanation among several of how they became a caste of pariahs. By the late Middle Ages there were thousands of them, spread out in small communities across Gascony, too many to have been only the descendants of lepers. Another explanation is that some were descended from soldiers in the retreating Saracen army, defeated at Poitiers. They may have been joined by later waves of Muslim refugees fleeing the *Reconquista* in Spain. Presumably at some time they converted to Christianity.

Some Cagots may have been Cathars, fleeing the carnage in the Languedoc when their beliefs in spiritual purity had them branded as heretics by the Pope and led to crusades against them. It is equally possible that a number of Jews joined the Cagots, at one time or another, to escape persecution.

In some descriptions of the Cagots they were short and sturdy with olive skin, in others they were tall, fair-haired and blue-eyed. The contradictory descriptions suggest no single ethnic origin. The fair-haired, blue-eyed Cagots can be explained as the descendants of the Visigoths, defeated by the Franks at the beginning of the sixth century. The Visigoths were more than a marauding army, they were a whole nation, and when their leaders and military classes fled over the Pyrenees, taking their servants with them, many of the middle classes were left behind in Gascony. The local population turned on their former oppressors and made them outcasts. If this explanation is true, the term of abuse *Canis Goths* or *Chien de Goth*, meaning dog of a Goth, may be the origin of the name Cagot.

The Visigoths made Toledo their capital and founded the first monarchy in the Iberian peninsula. They called this new land of theirs Spania, which evolved into modern Spain. The Cagot descendants of the Visigoths left behind in Gascony, when they wanted to reassure themselves that they were more than mere outcasts, there are tales of them using blocks of wood left over from their normal work to sculpt crowned heads that they would place near their front doors. When asked who the head represented, they would reply: 'It's my cousin, the King of Spain!'

Each of these explanations probably contains an element of truth, as successive generations of the marginalised and the dispossessed took refuge among the Cagots. Their struggle for integration was long and slow. In 1514 they petitioned Pope Leo X and in 1683 they paid dues for letters patent from Louis XIV, in each case with limited effect. In 1724, the Baron de Montesquieu intervened in favour of the rights of the Cagots of Biarritz.

After the Revolution the Cagots became assimilated into the general peasantry. The last identifiable Cagots lived on until the first quarter of the twentieth century, and they were finally lost sight of shortly after the First World War.

# FRUITS OF THE VINE

JACQUES-HENRI HAD AN APPRECIATION FOR THE FRUITS OF THE vine. He associated wine with friendship and the sharing of simple pleasures. It was a means of creating good humour rather than getting drunk. When he brought out a bottle from the store, he referred to it as *encore une bouteille de plaisir*.

Only Gascon wines were served at the Auberge. The local wines express the individualistic qualities of the vineyards and grape varieties, *le vrai goût du terroir*. There are full-bodied reds, clear fruity whites, easy-drinking rosés, sparkling *vins mousseux*, high-quality sweet *vins moelleux*, and of course the spirit of Gascony, Armagnac.

One concession to technology at the Auberge was a fax machine. Jacques-Henri wrote out a list of the wines and Armagnacs required and faxed the order down to a *négociant*, named Georges Castelbon, based in Boulogne-sur-Gesse. A day or two later Georges would appear in his ancient Citroën H-van, one of those big, square, angular vans that look as if they've been bolted together from old galvanised sheds, with suicide doors opening backwards. The engine whirred as it came up the drive, straining to pull its heavy load. On the side was a sign with the name of the *négociant* in faded wine-red letters arched over a bunch of grapes, George Castelbon & Cie, and underneath the simplest statement of his product: *Fruits de la Vigne*.

Georges was a real old-timer. He had a wealth of knowledge about wine and could talk about vines, vintages and vinification with enthusiasm and authority. He had been born in the village of Madiran, about fifty kilometres west of Péguilhan, was fiercely proud of his home soil, and supplied mainly Madiran wine to the Auberge.

I remember Georges drinking a glass of Madiran. '*Ah, ça me rappelle le pays!*' he said, suddenly getting quite emotional.

He took me to see a Madiran vineyard. It had been a hot summer, the vines were laden with grapes and the *vendange* would soon begin.

He came to pick me up at the farm at about five o'clock in the morning. As we drove westwards, the rising sun cast a long shadow of the van on the road in front of us. I was bleary-eyed and still half-asleep. The shadow gradually shortened as the sun rose higher in the sky behind us. We passed through shady valleys and over glorious hills. Georges swung the van along the winding roads, a little too fast for comfort downhill, slowly up the steeper hills, almost coming to a stop on some hairpin bends.

I heard the sudden explosive reports of gunfire in the woods, the sounds of hunters who had got up early to shoot ortolan and quail. We drove past a murderous-looking man standing by the roadside, wearing a fluorescent green jacket. He had bushy black sideburns sticking out from under his hunting hat and a shotgun slung over his arm. He was on patrol ready to shoot any animal that bolted onto the road. He touched his hat as we passed. We were safe, even if the animals were not.

We wound our way down into the valley of the river Adour, stopping at Maubourguet for a strong *café double* at a *relais* that had just opened for the morning.

Heading north, we turned off left and began the climb into the Madiran wine country, which covered the range of rolling hills above the sharp bend in the valley of the river Adour. I saw more and more land covered with vines. We passed through the village of Madiran, the shutters still closed on the windows of the houses along the main street. The Madiran hills looked subtly welcoming and peaceful. Just over the brow of a hill, we turned down a narrow road and through a pair of gates into the yard of the Château Vézac. We drove into the front yard of a neat-looking house, with outbuildings attached, looking out over a low stone wall and railings towards the vineyards of the *domaine*.

It was by then about seven o'clock in the morning. Monsieur Vézac, the *vigneron*, was already hard at work in the barn. When he heard the van he came out to greet us. *Salut, mon vieux*! Hello old friend. A small brown dog came with him, barking excitedly. Old Georges and Monsieur Vézac hadn't seen each other for three vintages, so there was a lot of hail-fellow-well-met hand shaking and back slapping to be done.

Georges introduced me as a *stagiaire* at the Auberge in Péguilhan, with an interest in wine making.

'Ah!' Monsieur Vézac exclaimed, 'isn't that the place run by Jacques-Henri Cazagnac? I've been told I should go there to try the *magret de canard*.'

I was surprised the reputation of the Auberge had reached this far.

'It's me who's cooking the *magrets* there at the moment,' I told Monsieur Vézac.

He looked rather taken aback, then he said, 'You've got talent, *jeune homme*!'

The conversation immediately turned to grapes. Monsieur Vézac wanted to show us round the vines before we enjoyed a tasting.

We walked out into the vineyards. The ground was pebbly soft clay, moist with dew. Strips of grass grew between the rows of vines, making them easy to walk around. The *domaine* was immaculately kept.

At the end of each row of vines was a red or pink rose bush, still in flower at the beginning of September, adding bright spots of colour. Rose bushes were planted next to the vines because they were more susceptible than grape vines to diseases like black rot and phylloxera. The roses acted as floral barometers, forewarning Monsieur Vézac of any disease, allowing him time to deal with the problem before it attacked the vines, when it would be too late.

The vines were heavily laden with bunches of grapes, hanging in tight clusters like purplish-black berries, with a glaucous bloom over the surface. Some of the leaves were beginning to turn their seasonal burnished copper colour. The vines looked very old. The stems were about twenty centimetres thick at the base and gnarled where they divided, and the grey-brown bark was coarse and flaky.

These were Tannat grapes, an indigenous Gascon variety, the backbone of strong, robust red Madiran wine. Tannat is a highly tannic grape – the clue is in the name! Tannins are the acidic compounds in the skin, pips and fragments of stalk, which make a wine taste harsh when it is young but give it depth with age. Madiran is a *vin de garde*, a wine to keep, and it has to be kept to allow those tannins to soften. Because of the high tannin levels,

Madiran is the only *appellation* in France that by official decree must be aged for at least one year. A good, strong Madiran will reach its best after five to ten years, longer in some cases. It is the most characteristic Gascon wine. As Monsieur Vézac said, *il sait bien porter le beret*, it knows how to wear a beret!

The white wines produced in the Madiran area are known by a different name, Pacherenc du Vic-Bilh. This unusual name comes from *pachec-en-rènc* – the local dialect for *piquets-en-rang*, meaning posts in a line, which describes the practice of training the vines over posts high above the ground, well above head height – and Vic-Bilh, meaning old hill villages. So the name means 'posts in a line from the old hill villages'. Local grape varieties are used, Arrufiac, Courbu, and especially Petit Manseng and Gros Manseng. Sweet Pacherenc is obtained from a late autumn harvest, *une vendange tardive*. The later the grapes are picked, the sweeter and more expensive the wine. The Madiran hills enjoy a gentle microclimate, perfect for making sweet wine: the air is moistened by Atlantic breezes in the spring, while the protective hills ensure low rainfall during the summer and autumn over the vine-yards on the south- and east-facing slopes.

Monsieur Vézac, Georges and I walked on to look at a row of Petit Manseng vines. The grapes were a fresh green colour, with a pink blush beneath the translucent skin. I cupped a bunch in the palm of my hand; they felt full and fruitful, and quite delicate. I picked a few to eat, which were deliciously sweet and fruity.

We walked through a tunnel of vines, which Monsieur Vézac and his wife had trained as a feature lead-ing up towards a belvedere, from where we could see the

211

whole *domaine*. Below us, the vineyards were held in the gentle curve of the hill. In the morning light the rows of vines shimmered like silken threads laid out carefully across the ground. I could feel the warm air beginning to rise up the slopes.

Above us, Château Vézac stood on top of the hill, looking out over its *domaine*. The château was an attractive, well-proportioned building, in the process of being refurbished, made of creamy-brown coloured stone with a horseshoe-shaped twin flight of steps in front. Monsieur Vézac and his wife lived in the smaller house by the yard.

I told Monsieur Vézac about my experience of grape picking the year before. He was impressed that I'd picked the Blanquette de Limoux grapes, and thought it was funny that I'd had to find out the hard way what tough work it was. I'd worked as a *coupeur*, I complained. The hardest part was having to squat. *Il faut s'accroupir*, we were ordered. We couldn't bend, which would hurt the back and meant we couldn't reach into the vines. We couldn't kneel, which would hurt the knees and was too slow. Squatting was such a painful position to maintain. My thigh muscles had ached and seized up. My face and arms were dirty and sticky from the dust and sap on the leaves. The only time we moved out of the squatting position was to tip our buckets into the *hotte* at the end of the row.

Monsieur Vézac smiled and assured me that at Château Vézac, all the grapes were picked by machine. The harvesting machines pick the grapes quickly, he explained, which is better for a consistent vintage.

The wine cellar, *le chai*, was the whole basement of the château, three cavernous rooms with vaulted ceilings.

New oak barrels with shining steel bands stood in rows, two tiers high. Light came in through a few small high windows set in the thick cellar walls and from new halogen lamps set into the stone floor. Monsieur Vézac was very proud of the newly refurbished cellar. He explained that the thick walls and small windows maintained a constant temperature in winter or summer, without any artificial heating or cooling, which was absolutely necessary for aging good wine. In those rows of barrels the wine was going through its slow, silent aging, as the tannins from the grapes achieved a synthesis with the tannins from the wood.

We walked back down the hill. The fronts of the barns were open and everything inside was neatly and tidily stored: a small tractor, spraying equipment, crates, pipes and spare barrels. Taking up most of the space in one barn was a giant old wooden wine press, no longer used, with a huge rusting iron screw sticking up in the middle.

The tasting room was in a converted barn next to the house. In the middle stood a stunning circular glass-topped table with a base made from gnarled old vine stems, buffed and varnished.

Monsieur Vézac took three wine glasses from a shelf. We tried a pure Tannat red, a short-and-sturdy beret-wearing Gascon wine, the darkest ruby-red colour, strong and smooth – a real connoisseur's wine, not for the faint-hearted.

We ate some nougat to clean our palates and then tasted some Pacherenc dry. Fruity and invigorating, it seemed to evoke the clear, refreshing air of the hills where the grapes are grown. There was an aftertaste I couldn't identify, until Monsieur Vézac told me it was a hint of *pierre à fusil*, gun flint.

We rounded off our tasting session with some sweet Pacherenc *moelleux*, honeyed and smooth, not cloying, with subtle hints of caramelised pear, citrus and spicy in the finish. There was something powerful but subtle about the sweetness of the wine, which gave a feeling of contentment. I was impressed.

It was only mid-morning and the wine was making my head spin. Monsieur Vézac and Georges seemed unaffected by it. They had some discussion about the weather, the soil, the imminent harvest and vinification techniques.

As Georges and I drove off I thought how very lucky Monsieur Vézac and his family were to own those vineyards in that idyllic setting, devoting their lives to cultivating the vines and producing good wine. They worked hard and saw the fruits of their labour all around them.

On the way back, Georges and I stopped at the *Tonnellerie* near the village, so that he could show me where the barrels were made. It was an unusual-shaped wooden building, with a roof that came right down to the ground on one side, and a high wall with big sliding doors on the other. We parked in the yard and pulled on the handle of one of the sliding doors, where someone had written *TIREZ* in marker pen.

Inside the *Tonnellerie* was dark, with a brazier glowing at the far end and narrow shafts of light coming down from high windows. The smell of wood was very strong. The barrel maker, the *tonnelier*, saw us come in, put down his tools and came over to greet us. He wore a tough leather apron and thick leather gloves. His handshake had a grip like a vice. He had never shown an Englishman around his *Tonnellerie* before.

214

He took us through the stages of barrel making. At one end of the workshop staves of wood were stacked under the low roof. On the top surface they looked dark, but when he turned one over it was silver coloured underneath. All the wood was oak. The trees were two hundred years old, felled in the dead of winter, under a waning moon, when the tree was resting and the sap had settled. The wood was seasoned for between twenty-six and thirty months. The first stage of making the barrel was to shape the staves into tapered sections. These were bound with metal hoops at one end, then the barrel was soaked and cooked so that the wood could be bent into the curved shape of the barrel and the hoops fitted over the other end. The barrels were toasted over an open fire, the flames just licking the inside, creating a fine charred layer on the inner walls. The toasting added flavour to the wine: a light toasting for white wine, a longer toasting for red. The final stage was to hammer in the top and bottom, and there it was, the finished *barrique*.

'I can finish perhaps two barrels a day,' the barrel maker told us. 'There aren't many artisan barrel makers left in Gascony. Most barrels are now mass-produced in factories; they can easily turn out a hundred and fifty a day. They are the Renaults of barrel making.'

Renault was a byword for mass-production.

'I have to make other things to survive,' the barrel maker continued, pointing to some items near the door. 'These barrels will be a set of chairs when I've cut them in half, and this thing here, with the tap on top, this is a beer pump.'

The trip to the vineyard and the barrel maker's was timely and memorable. Gascony had enjoyed a mild, wet spring, soaking the ground, followed by a long, hot, dry summer, forcing the vines to do their best work. The harvest started early. The grapes were rich and strong. The Madiran wines of that year were some of the best red wines of Gascony from the end of the century. Even now, some of that vintage are just reaching their peak of maturity.

# THIS PRECIOUS BOOTY

WHEN I THINK OF JACQUES-HENRI, I THINK OF ARMAGNAC, the two became so closely associated in my mind. He didn't drink a lot, but he held it close to his heart.

Armagnac – *ce précieux butin*, this precious booty – has an aura of mystery about it. No one knows exactly when the drink was first made. Distillation processes were known in early mediaeval Europe, for the purpose of distilling herbs for medicine. The best guess is that Armagnac was first produced at the beginning of the fourteenth century, more than two hundred years before anyone thought of doing a similar thing in Cognac.

The name comes from a Frankish knight named Herremann, who was granted a fiefdom in the southwest by King Clovis towards the end of the fifth century. Herremann meant strong warrior: it was later Latinised into Arminius, and then Gasconised into Armagnac. The spirit was originally known as *aigardent* or *eau ardente*, meaning firewater; only later did it take the name of the land where it was produced, the home of those troublesome, ill-fated Counts of Armagnac.

The Armagnac vineyards occupy a vine-leaf-shaped area in the centre of Gascony. The grape varieties are the versatile Ugni Blanc, the delicate Folle Blanche and the aromatic Colombard. There are as many subtle variations of Armagnac as there are small, independent producers. The vineyards are grouped in three *appellations*. The most productive is the Bas-Armagnac area to the west, with its sandy soils. It produces light and fruity Armagnac, known as Black Armagnac, from its association with the nearby forests. The La Ténarèze *appellation* in the centre produces vigorous, aromatic Armagnacs. The Haut-Armagnac *appellation* to the east and south is a large *terroir* producing small quantities of high-quality spirit, known as White Armagnac because of the chalky soil in the area.

The distinction between Bas and Haut describes the lie of the land rather than the quality of the Armagnac. The whole of the territory enjoys a good climate: the pine forests of the Landes shelter it from the worst of the Atlantic weather, and when a steady wind blows from the west the faint scent of pine resin is carried in the air.

The mysterious transmutation of wine into spirit takes place in alembic stills. Different types have been used, outlawed, then reintroduced at different times. Portable stills – ambulating alembics – continue to be used, travelling from farm to farm, allowing farmers to make their own Armagnac. If anything appeals to a Gascon, it is something that allows him to be independent.

The spirit is perfectly clear when it comes out of the still. The oak barrels impart the distinctive rich colours and flavours. Armagnac is aged for its first three years in new Monlezun black oak casks. After three years, it is transferred to older barrels that have already lost much of their flavour, in this way slowing down the rate of absorption of the tannins from the wood and ensuring the gentler qualities of the drink. During the aging process, which may last for decades, some of the alcohol evaporates. This lost portion is known as *la part des anges*, the angels' share.

Armagnac is reputed to have medicinal properties. Jacques-Henri said, with a nudge and a wink, that it helped to preserve his youthful vitality, and to emphasise the point he added, '*Ça reveille les morts!*' It may not have supernatural powers to bring the dead back to life, but its magic works on the palate, where a momentary sharpness melts into a smooth, gentle warmth. The aromas of Armagnac are complex: apricot, prune, fig, rose, violet, vanilla, liquorice, treacle, tobacco, chestnut, clove, honey, ginger and hawthorn, the most sacred tree for the ancient Vascones. The drink has a delicate, captivating sweetness, called *le rancio*, which makes it the perfect *digestif* for settling the stomach after a meal. Gascons will sometimes swallow a nip between courses during a heavy meal, to help clear the palate and create a hole for more food, *le trou gascon*.

Jacques-Henri recited to me the Armagnac prayer, which certainly showed his priorities in life:

*Mon Dieu, donne-moi la santé pour longtemps,*
*De l'amour de temps en temps,*
*Du travail pas souvent,*
*Mais de l'Armagnac à chaque instant.*

Dear God, give me long good health,
Some love from time to time,
Work not too often,
But Armagnac at every moment.

Some connoisseurs insist that Armagnac be drunk from tulip-shaped glasses, which concentrate the aroma. Jacques-Henri wasn't at all fussy about his Armagnac.

When he wasn't taking crafty swigs out of the bottle, he was happy to drink from tumblers. This was the Auberge, not the Château.

Various types of bottles are used for Armagnac and there are different opinions over which is the more authentic. The tall, straight bottle, known as *la droite*, is the simplest to store and pour, but the shape is also known as the *cognacaise*, not a good association. For the died-in-the-wool Gascon patriot, Armagnac should come instead in the flat, pear-shaped and slightly misshapen bottle known as *la basquaise*. Oversize bottles of Armagnac are impressive, like the one-and-a-half-litre magnum. I knew I was well in with Jacques-Henri when he brought out the formidable two-and-a-half-litre *pot gascon* from the larder.

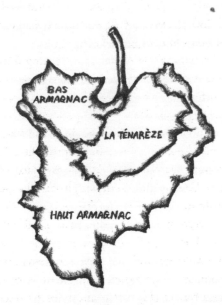

# PASTIS AND PEANUTS

THE VANNEUSE, THE GRAIN-WINNOWING MACHINE IN THE BARN
that had caused me so much pain, broke down. I was
secretly pleased about this. Jacques-Henri wasn't
able to mend it himself, so he called in Gaston, the local
fixer.

Gaston was from the neighbouring village of Saint-
Ferréol. There was something distinctly louche about
him. He came on a Sunday morning with his girlfriend,
who was about half his age and dressed from head to toe
in black. Gaston worked noisily on the machine, while she
stood around not speaking to anyone, petulantly drilling
her big toe into the ground. She obviously had other plans
for that Sunday morning.

The wrenching, clattering and grunting finished and
the machine was fixed. Jacques-Henri paid Gaston for the
work and offered to buy him a drink. There was going to
be a live performance of the *cornemuse* or French bagpipe in
the Péguilhan café that afternoon; there had been posters
on the wooden board outside for a fortnight announcing
the forthcoming attraction. All of us – me, Jacques-Henri,
Paul, Bruno, Gaston and his sulky girlfriend – decided to
go to the café to hear the performance.

There were many more cars than usual parked outside the café. We walked in, saluted everyone, shook hands
with people we knew and sat at the only remaining empty
table. As soon as we settled in, we ordered pastis with jugs
of water and bowls of salted peanuts. Pastis is a working

man's drink. When water is poured in it changes colour from a dull, clear greenish-yellow to a bright, opaque cream. We ate salted peanuts with our drinks, the salt on the peanuts countering the sharp flavour of the aniseed.

A lot of people from around the village, mostly men, had come to hear the *cornemuse*. They talked loudly with their friends and neighbours as the café filled up. I recognised a lot of people. The sign fixer who'd thought Anja and I were Vikings was talking animatedly to Monsieur Fustignac. He saluted us and made a hammering motion with his arm, to show the work he remembered us by. The postman who never got out of his van was there – he did have legs after all! Hans was there without Lotte, knocking back the pastis. The old farmer whose cows Paul and I had nearly crashed into was in the café, as was Youssef, the master of the *méchoui*, although he wasn't drinking. I also recognised the family of mad farmers from across the valley. Madame Parle-Beaucoup was run off her feet – for once she had no time to talk.

At the back of the room was a great brown plastic wine tank, with a tap at the bottom, where people could fill their glass or their *pichet*. One customer was in high spirits. He bent over backwards, holding his head under the tap, pretending to drink from it, and promptly fell over. His friends at the next table laughed – '*Bah, le con!*', what an idiot – and threw peanuts at him.

Gaston had comments to make about nearly everything. He screwed up his eyes as he talked, looking shiftily at people as if he was trying to judge the effect of what he was saying. He thought it was funny to comment on the madness of the English driving on the other side of the road: '*Ils sont fous ces Anglais, ils roulent à gauche!*' He scrounged cigarettes off everyone in turn: '*T'aurais pas une clope?*' You haven't got a fag? He was trying to sell his old banger of a car and he even asked me if I wanted to buy it, saying it would be useful for me to drive home in. I pointed out that, as he said, we drive on the left, so the steering wheel would be on the wrong side when I got home.

'Hey,' he replied, 'you can drive it as far as the ferry port and just leave it there.'

I declined the offer.

Gaston was set on impressing the English *Godon*. He told me that he knew someone who knew Maurice Prat, the less famous brother of Jean Prat, Gascony's most famous rugby player.

'Who?'

'*Le rugbyman!*'

At the time I'd never heard of either of the Prat brothers. Jean Prat was a living legend in Gascony: he led the French team to historic victories over *les Anglais* at Twickenham in the 1950s, earning himself the titles Mister Rugby and Sir John.

'Do you know why horses don't eat oysters?' Gaston asked me, wanting to impress me further with his Gascon humour.

'No.'

'So that Gascons can keep their feet warm.'

'How's that?'

'A Gascon walks into an *auberge* on a winter's evening, feeling the cold. All the places around the fire are taken. The Gascon says to the serving boy, "Go out to the stable and give my horse two dozen oysters." The boy is surprised but does what he is told. All the travellers rush outside with him to watch the horse eat the oysters. While they're outside the Gascon settles himself into the best seat by the fire. The travellers come back inside and tell him that the horse won't eat the oysters. "What?" exclaims the Gascon, toasting his toes, "my horse won't eat the oysters? Very well then, I'll eat them myself!"'

At last, the *cornemuse* player arrived. He set himself up at the end of the room. He fitted perfectly the image of the country musician, aged about thirty, with serious eyes and long, dark hair in a ponytail, a sort of modern-day minstrel.

He began to inflate the *cornemuse*. It was unlike anything I'd seen before or since. The traditional Gascon bagpipe is *en peau de chèvre*, made from a whole goatskin turned inside-out, with the head and feet removed. Red and gold tassels were tied tightly around the leg stumps to block the holes. The mouthpiece was inserted into the chest where the oesophagus would once have been. The chanter pipe came out of the neck. It took a few minutes to blow the skin up fully. Inflated, the instrument took on the size and shape of a goat. It was grotesque. I thought, if he blows hard enough it might jump up and run away of its own accord.

There was something strangely exotic about the *cornemuse*. I was reminded of pictures I'd seen of *buzkashi*, the type of polo they play in Afghanistan, where horsemen tussle with each other over a headless goat carcass.

The *cornemuse* player looked entirely at ease with his bizarre instrument, which was almost too big for him to hold under his arm. The room quietened down in anticipation as he prepared himself. There was spontaneous applause from everyone when he finally pressed his elbow into the side of the goat belly and started to play. The *cornemuse* had a deep, low timbre, with haunting under-tones reminiscent of North Africa. The strangest thing was to hear any melodious sound at all coming from a headless, footless, inflated goatskin.

After several increasingly reluctant encores, the musician was getting tired of blowing into the skin to keep it inflated. When the audience asked him for yet more tunes, he protested with a line which I suspect may be a commonplace among *cornemuse* players: '*Si vous voulez une chanson, écoutez le vent, il les connaît toutes.*' If you want a song, listen to the wind, it knows them all.

The air became thick with pungent tobacco smoke and the smell of aniseed. Relaxing in the café, drinking pastis, listening to the *cornemuse* – this really was *la paysandaille*, a troupe of peasants in their element, enjoying themselves. At village gatherings like this the local people expressed *l'amour du vieux pays natal*, their love for the old land where they were born. Sitting with them, treated almost as one of their own, I felt like an honorary Gascon. Some of the men were still wearing their blue work over-alls, a reminder that even though it was Sunday, farmers don't have a day off. The men would go back to work when the break was over.

I walked on my own through the village back to the Auberge, to clear my head. The weather was still, the ani-mals quiet – there was an embracing silence all around. The air smelled sweet, apart from a faint whiff of *caca d'oie* coming from the goose farm. In the distance I could clearly see the Pyrenees. The mountains were always there, a grey, white or purple shadow along the southern horizon.

Centuries ago, pilgrims passed through Gascony on the road to Santiago de Compostella. A twelfth-century guide written for pilgrims, the *Codex de Compostelle*, described the Gascons as poor but generous, and always hospitable towards travellers. For mediaeval pilgrims making the journey on foot, Boulogne-sur-Gesse was a regular stopping-off place. In the nineteenth century, other pilgrims began flocking to Gascony for the healing waters at Lourdes. For the modern traveller, the country-side of Gascony possesses its own soothing balm for the soul. The charm of the landscape and the pleasant attitude of the people invite you to linger and return.

Gascony is a beautiful land. Gascony is also a state of mind, existing somewhere in the warm south, a place of simplicity, plenty and fulfilment.

# AU REVOIR

THE LONG, HOT SUMMER WAS DRAWING TO A CLOSE. THE earth had produced a bountiful harvest and was resting in the late summer sunshine, getting ready for another season of plenty. The land, content with itself, looked drowsy and dreamy. Sunflowers were blackening in the fields as they ripened and dried ready to be harvested. At the far end of the village, an elderly woman could be seen brushing up acorns from her drive, to feed as treats to her pigs. The season was maturing, and I had grown with it.

The end of my stay in Gascony was in sight. I knew I would have to return home before too long for the start of the autumn term. It had been a perfect summer, more rewarding than I could possibly have imagined. I felt truly alive and in tune with everything around me. The sunshine, fresh air and healthy food had left me glowing inside and out. The Auberge had become a home-from-home. I liked the sense of camaraderie that came from working together.

Some of the work had been hard and dirty. Shovelling heaps of compacted sheep droppings may not be everyone's idea of fun and killing a sheep may seem a brutal act, but I was pleased with myself for having done them. I was young enough to take part in everything, to embrace the whole situation, but just old enough to appreciate the value of life in Gascony. I had gone with ideas but they weren't fixed ideas, and so in Jacques-Henri's immortal words, I was able to adapt myself. It had been worth making the effort to get used to the southwest accent, with its rich, warm, expressive tones: it brought me closer to the people and the way they thought. Living among the country folk of Gascony, sharing their work, their pleasures and their day-to-day concerns, had taught me so much. This was the simple life. I saw how it was possible to live without things – like electronic gadgets and exotic holidays – that many people think are necessities. There was a strict routine in the way they planned their work and their leisure, always in one way or another tied to the land and the seasons. I was beginning to feel the pull of the land and the sense of obligation towards it that these people felt.

Meeting Anja had made my stay in Gascony even more fulfilling, and we wanted to have some time to ourselves before the summer was over. Towards the end of September we told Jacques-Henri we would be leaving very soon. We felt awkward, as if we were committing an act of desertion. The news seemed to surprise and upset Jacques-Henri, but he tried not to show his disappointment. In a businesslike way he said he would settle our final payments. He had wanted me to stay on a while longer: there was end-of-season work to be done on the farm – cutting back, tilling, storing and repairing – and I would have come in useful. Nonetheless, Anja and I both felt we were leaving on a high note.

The evening before our departure, Marie-Jeanne served a farewell meal of stuffed wild pigeons, *palombes farcies*, shot that very morning by a skilled *paloumeyre* from the village, who carried decoy pigeons tethered to a stick to attract the wild birds. We had one whole stuffed pigeon each, wrapped in strips of bacon. As an accompaniment we had sautéed *cèpe* mushrooms, gathered in the woods, which added a woody flavour to the dish. *Cep* means tree trunk in Gascon, and their thick stalks did indeed look like tree trunks. They brought home the idea of autumn as a time for going back to the roots of things and taking stock of the harvest. Fruit was well in season, and for dessert we had stewed *pêches de vigne*, small peaches that grew on low trees beside the drive up to the Auberge. After the farewell meal we solemnly drank a round of Armagnac, to mark the end of our employment as *stagiaires*, raising our glasses in a toast: 'À *la toa*!… À *la toa*!…'

Jacques-Henri didn't say much after the toast. Marie-Jeanne was kindly concerned that we would have a safe journey. Paul and Bruno wished us well. Nicolas seemed truly disappointed we were leaving. *Au revoir* Monsieur Martin!

On the morning we left, I packed my things in my rucksack and brushed out my room at the farm, pausing to take one last look around. Jacques-Henri was pleased by this: he said I really was a gentleman-farmer after all. The turquoise espadrilles he'd given me the day I arrived were falling apart, and I had to throw them away.

Standing on the front doorstep we bade our farewells to the family. Paul had his arm around Florence's waist. Marie-Jeanne, as soon as she'd said goodbye, returned to the kitchen where she was starting to prepare the lunchtime menu – the Auberge would go on without us. Pattes came bounding out from the dappled shade under the trees. He pushed his head against me and I knelt down and rubbed his chest, by way of a goodbye. He wagged his magnificent fan tail, oblivious to the fact that we were about to leave.

Jacques-Henri gave us a lift in the Renault. We stopped en route to say *auf Wiedersehen* to Hans and Lotte. We could see two hands and two feet, not belonging to the same person, sticking up above the artichokes. Hans and Lotte were practising yoga, but they turned themselves the right way up to say goodbye. Then Jacques-Henri drove us down to the bus stop on the main road, where we'd watched the Tour de France what seemed like a long time ago. He heaved our rucksacks out of the boot and shook our hands brusquely, then to our surprise produced a bottle of Armagnac as a leaving present. The last we saw of him was the white car turning up the narrow road towards Péguilhan. He waved but did not look back.

The bus took us all the way to Toulouse, about an hour's journey away. Along the route it pulled in and out of a succession of small towns and villages. Locals got on and off, and some of them looked curiously at the two strangers sitting at the back. With our rucksacks on the seats in front of us we must have looked like real back-packers – *de vrais sac-à-dos-istes*! In the central square in Lombez, a group of beret-topped old men were standing around chatting in the corner of the *pétanque* course, under the plane trees, bantering and no doubt putting the world to rights. They stopped talking to see who got on and off the bus.

We arrived at our destination, the *Gare Routière* in Toulouse, at about lunchtime.

'I hope we haven't turned into country bumpkins,' said Anja, as we got off the bus.

Two thousand years ago, the ancient settlement of Tolosa was the bridge point for the Roman invasion of Aquitaine. The river Garonne was the frontier between the Aquitanians and the Gauls. Later it became the border between Gascony and the rest of France. When Anja and I had each made our separate ways to Péguilhan at the start of the summer, Toulouse had been an important stage on our way into Gascony. Now on our way back, it felt as though it was the symbolic gateway to the outside world. It was good that we were passing through together.

Anja had been to Toulouse before and she suggested we head for the Place du Capitole. We made our way through winding mediaeval streets, in the shadow of tall, ancient town houses, with crumbling walls of reddish-pink bricks and yellow stone. At each crossroads we walked into squares of sunlight. Then suddenly we emerged into the grandiose heart of the city. For a moment the open square made us pause. One side was dominated by the imposing classical façade of the Capitole building. The others were lined with arcades of chic boutiques, cafés, restaurants and grand hotels. It was lunchtime: the square was busy and the café terraces were full. There were businessmen in shirtsleeves, smartly dressed Toulousaines engaged in serious shopping, and students everywhere. The atmosphere was vibrant and energetic.

We could see why Toulouse is known as *la ville rose*, most of its buildings were pink. The Capitole was faced with rose-pink bricks and pale pink marble columns. Even the pavements were pink, whether they were dyed tarmac or coloured stone. The effect was a subtle, ambient pink light throughout the city.

We sat at a table under the grid of big, square parasols in front of the café Le Florida. This seemed to be where the stylish came to see and be seen. When the waiter deigned to serve us, we said we would like ice cream. He insisted we try the speciality violet variety.

There is a charming story behind the violets of Toulouse. They are a particular strain, a highly fragrant variety called *la violette Parme de Toulouse*, grown in the hills outside the city. The story goes that the first flower came to the city a couple of centuries ago, when a soldier from Toulouse, serving in the army in Italy, returned home with a violet as a present for his sweetheart. She planted the violet and, when it grew, she took cuttings and gave them to friends and neighbours; gradually more and more people grew violets, all from that first little plant. In time an industry developed around the violet, and the people of Toulouse adopted the flower as their emblem. Brides getting married in the Capitole typically carry a posy of violets.

Our ice cream was a true violet colour, perfumed and smooth, speckled with tiny, gritty pieces of crystallized petals. We ate slowly, savouring the moment and taking in the scene. This was the perfect place for people watching; after all, in Péguilhan there had been very few people to watch.

Anja and I spent the rest of the afternoon and the evening in Toulouse, waiting for the night train to Paris. With nothing particular to do, we walked down to the river and whiled away the carefree hours lolling on the grass of the Quai de la Daurade, looking out over the broad, sweeping curve of the Garonne. Toulousains strolled along the riverbank path, stopping here and there to admire the view. A few cyclists whirred quietly by. The ripples on the water glittered in the sunlight like scattered diamonds.

A man dressed as a harlequin walked up to us, handing out flyers for a restaurant called L'Arlequin. The vivid colours of his diamond-patterned costume jarred with the muted pinks, greens and blues of the riverbank. He presented us with a flyer, then took off his hat and bowed with an exaggerated flourish. We thanked him and promised we would go to his restaurant that evening. He grinned with just one half of his face.

'*À la bonne heure, mes amis, à la bonne heure,*' he said as he tiptoed theatrically away, like a mischievous character in a play.

I crumpled the flyer into my back pocket, and in spite of our promise we forgot about the restaurant.

With our feet dangling above the river, I poured a slug of Armagnac into a plastic travel beaker and we shared it a sip at a time. The warmth of the spirit coursed through our veins. We half-closed our eyes and sat until the light faded and the Gascon sun had slipped behind the Toulouse skyline.

'Look,' said Anja softly, pointing to the streetlamps on the bridge, fitted with pink covers that hung like pennants. The pink light of the lamps replaced the glow of the sun. 'They think of everything.'

Late in the evening, we walked to Matabiau station and boarded the overnight train for Paris. We hadn't thought to reserve couchettes for the eight-hour journey; they were all fully booked and we had to make do with ordinary seats. For the first few hours we shared a compartment with a man who sat in silence. He made us feel uncomfortable. The train stopped somewhere in the middle of the night – we didn't notice the name of the station – the man got off and we were left to ourselves for the rest of the journey.

Peering between the orange pleated curtains at the darkness outside, we watched the country racing by in the night shadows. We saw hills in outline beneath an indigo sky. Anja's cheek brushed gently against mine. We felt excited and free. Curling up together on the seat, lulled by the rolling of the carriage and the steely roar of the wheels, we eventually fell asleep. The next thing we knew we were being woken in the morning by the jolts of the train as it crossed the points approaching the Gare d'Austerlitz.

In Paris the air was crisp and fresh. We climbed the hill up to the Place de la Contrescarpe, which for us held the charm of a small provincial town square in the midst of the metropolis. The fountain spouted and sparkled, shopkeepers briskly washed down the pavements in front of their premises, people walked past on their way to work – the city was coming to life around us. We had breakfast on the terrace of the Café la Chope on the angle of the square. Inside, the coffee machine spluttered and hissed behind the counter. We heard the gentle clatter of cutlery on plates and saucers as the waiter brought our breakfast out to our table, creamy coffee and soft *brioches parisiennes*. Anja's eyes were a misty pearl blue in the early morning light and her face was radiant. I took a mental snapshot of her sitting across from me.

'What are you doing?' she asked.

'I'm taking your picture, so that I never forget this.'

She smiled serenely and looked down at her coffee. The moment was perfect.

We spent a few days in Paris, at a nice, bright hotel in a quiet street off the Rue des Écoles, on the edge of the Latin Quarter. We stayed for as long as our money lasted. On our last morning, with a few hours to spare before we took our separate trains to different countries, we went on a final walk through the city. Somewhere near the abbey of Saint-Germain-des-Prés, where the streets became quieter and the shops more select, we stopped to look at the sumptuous window display of a grand old chocolate shop: Debauve & Gallais. *Maison fondée en* 1800 ~ *Fournisseurs des anciens rois de France*. House founded in 1800 ~ Purveyors to the former kings of France.

This was our last day and we were feeling extravagant. As we went inside, a bell tinkled quietly over the door. It was like entering another world: polished wood panelling, marble columns, gleaming mirrors. Debauve & Gallais's premises were a temple to chocolate. We stood bedazzled before a half-moon glass counter, looking at lavish displays. Small signs with copperplate gold lettering stated the country of origin of the cocoa used for each type of chocolate: Ecuador, Ghana, Madagascar...

The female assistant, immaculately dressed in a grey uniform and a hairnet, smiled attentively.

'*Madame, Monsieur, vous désirez?*' she asked, pretending not to notice that we didn't look like her usual customers.

We weren't sure what to reply at first, we were so struck by the contrast between this luxury and the simple life we'd been living in the country. But the rich smell of the chocolate and the opulence of the display were seductive. We picked out some *pistoles*, flat, round chocolates like big old coins, with flecks of gold leaf set into the upper surface. We had just enough money for a dozen. The assistant carefully packed them in an exquisite gift box, royal blue and pale grey, embossed with the shop's emblem, a blue-and-gold oval shield adorned with a gold crown and *fleurs-de-lis*.

Anja remarked that the shop was very beautiful. The assistant told us it had been designed by the architects whom Napoleon had chosen to create the retreat at Malmaison for the Empress Joséphine. All we could do was nod and look suitably impressed.

As we walked out of the *chocolaterie*, it began to rain heavily. We took shelter outside a café on the Boulevard Saint-Germain. The rain drummed on the ivory-coloured awning above us and bounced off the pavement at our feet. Standing out of the rain, we fed each other nibbles of chocolate and gold. The cars swished through the rain, throwing up clouds of spray, stopping and starting to the sequence of the traffic lights, like metallic waves ebbing and flowing to the rhythm of the city.

We took the Métro to the Gare de l'Est, where Anja boarded her train back to Germany. We lingered out our goodbye in the doorway of the carriage as other people climbed aboard, jostling us with their shoulders as they mounted the steps. Down the platform, a whistle blew.

'Anja, promise me we'll keep in touch,' I insisted.

'I promise,' she said, folding her arms around my neck.

The guard came along closing the doors and reluctantly I stepped down onto the platform. Anja leant out of the window and waved as the train slowly pulled away. I waved back until she disappeared from sight.

I walked across the city to the Gare Saint-Lazare, where my train to Dieppe was due to leave in a couple of hours. It was raining more gently, a warm, steady drizzle after the downpour. The rain heralded the last stage of my journey home to England and gave me a foretaste of the weather I was going to have to get used to again.

I came back to England on the night ferry. The boat docked in Newhaven at dawn. The engine rumbled deep inside the ferry as it pulled alongside. Seagulls shrieked as they circled overhead. In the shivery sea air I felt calm and as I looked back across the Channel, I recalled a few lines from Matthew Arnold's poem 'Dover Beach':

> ...on the French coast, the light
> Gleams, and is gone; the cliffs of England stand,
> Glimmering and vast, out in the tranquil bay.

Slipping behind the approaching autumn was a golden summer, which had been how all summers should be. I put my hand in my pocket and found the acorn I'd picked up from the drive in front of the Auberge the morning we left. It made me think about what would be happening back at the Auberge and the farm. Cazagnac family life would be continuing without us. Any moment now the cockerel would be giving the village its early-morning wake-up call. Marie-Jeanne would soon be preparing breakfast, and Jacques-Henri would be leading the sheep out into the fields, without me to help. Pattes would be wondering where I'd gone. I imagined Monsieur Fustignac getting up early to polish his tractor. Hans and Lotte would be out in their garden facing the rising sun, practising their first yoga of the day, and the sun would be streaming through the cast windows of the Auberge. It might be raining in England, but in my mind's eye, in that enchanted place on a hilltop in Gascony, the Auberge would always be bathed in sunshine.

At the end of the season the old building would be settling down for a well-earned rest. The refurbishment of the *gîtes* was complete. This had been only the second year the Auberge had been open for business and the first year it had been fully functioning. I was pleased that I'd been there near the start, and hoped I'd made a good contribution to its future prosperity. Mighty oaks from little acorns grow. I thought about the autumn tasks Jacques-Henri had wanted me to do, pruning, digging, tidying, shovelling, new challenges for the new season – I knew in my heart that one day I would return.

# EPILOGUE

ANJA AND I KEPT OUR PROMISE TO STAY IN TOUCH. WE EVEN met up a few times, in London, Paris and Heidelberg. We wrote to each other as well; this was before emails and text messages killed off the habit of writing letters.

For a few years I concentrated on building a career. I lived in Paris for a year, but I didn't go back to Gascony. I remembered that summer as a unique and magical time, like a golden capsule, somehow separate from the rest of life. Then unexpectedly, Anja sent me a letter with a cutting from a German newspaper, a feature article on the gastronomic delights of Gascony, showcasing in particular the Auberge at Péguilhan. Illustrating the article was a photo of Jacques-Henri! There he was, raising his wine-glass in a welcoming salute and smiling cheerfully with the same old twinkle in his eye. Suddenly, I felt an over-whelming wave of warmth and affection for Gascony and an irresistible desire to return.

A few months later, as I drove up through the double hairpin bend leading to the village, I passed the sign for Péguilhan and smiled at the familiar name. When I reached the Auberge, good memories came flooding back. Why had I taken so long to return? It felt like coming home. The flowers and shrubs around the buildings were more plentiful than ever. The children's swing was still in the clearing in the trees. It felt strange to return as a guest rather than a *stagiaire*.

There have been some surprising changes. Jacques-Henri is no longer there, so I never saw him again. The farm has been sold and Marie-Jeanne runs the Auberge. The eldest son, Paul, has a family and is waiting to take over the business. The Auberge has been extended to the side, creating a large kitchen and a spacious restaurant and function room. Nevertheless, in some respects it hasn't changed at all. The treads on the rickety old wooden staircase still feel as though they might give way underfoot, and the bedrooms are exactly as they were.

*Stagiaires* are not employed any more, instead apprentices are taken on as part of the government's work training scheme for young people. The Auberge provides work experience for the *brevet*, the professional qualification in the hotel and catering industry, and of course the French government contributes towards the costs. I asked one young woman working for Marie-Jeanne in the restaurant how long her placement lasted.

'Two years!' she sighed, resignedly, making it sound like a very long time, and so it probably seemed for a lively young person from Toulouse to live so deep in the countryside.

Pattes has long since passed away. There are a couple of dogs in the village who resemble him, with big paws and fan tails; they bound up to greet visitors in the same friendly manner. I'd like to think he had his way with some of the local female dogs and left his offspring behind.

The changes to Péguilhan since I first went there are a story of growth and inward investment rather than real change. The village now has a bus service and a post box, and the *Mairie* has been given an arcaded stone façade, making it look like a *bastide*-cum-*hacienda*. Hans and Lotte have sold their eccentric blue house and moved on. I hope their Mercedes is still running, wherever they are. The village café has closed. I was told that Monsieur Fustignac had died, so Madame Parle-Beaucoup and her husband later sold up and moved to a retirement home in Boulogne-sur-Gesse. I was amused to learn that the night-club La Guinguette – and I still can't pinpoint where it is – is still going strong after several closures and reopenings.

The houses in the village are being bought and reno-vated by local people rather than outsiders. The old ruin where Anja and I picked blackberries has been demol-ished and there are new bungalows on the site. The village primary school has a full intake and the happy sound of children's voices in the playground can be heard through-out the village. There is a zebra crossing on the road out-side the school – protection for the children, but somehow out of place across a road that has no pavements and only sees one or two vehicles an hour drive slowly past.

Down on the main road in the valley is some light industry, relieving the local economy's complete reliance on farming. There is even a boulangerie for the workers. When I was there Marie-Jeanne baked her own bread, and other people depended on the bread van coming round every other day, with a limited selection of loaves. Now the Péguilhanais have only a twenty-minute walk or a five-minute drive to the boulangerie. Some workers from the factories come up to the Auberge for a hearty lunch. This is home-grown prosperity: their Gascon way of life will go on.

Revisiting the Auberge was the inspiration for me to begin exploring the rest of Gascony. I have travelled throughout the region since then, from the *cirques* of the

Pyrenees to the wide, open beaches and Atlantic breakers of the *côte d'argent*; from the vineyards of Armagnac to the oyster beds of the Bassin d'Arcachon; from the plum orchards of the Agenais to the pine forests of the Landes. I have seen marsh shepherds walking on stilts and animal-friendly bullfights, where teams of people acrobatically dodge cows instead of bulls and no cows get hurt. They use the same cows year on year, and so the second or third time round the animals have wised up to the game. Throughout my travels, I have consistently chosen not to have my photo taken next to the road sign at Condom.

Some things *are* changing. In the Gers in central Gascony, British second-homers have found an alternative to Provence and the Dordogne and are buying up and restoring any ramshackle farmhouse, barn or cowshed the locals are happy to sell to them. In the larger markets, in Condom, Auch and Eauze, English voices are frequently heard. There's a curious parallel between the current influx of home buyers from abroad looking for the good life in the sun, and the settlers in the Middle Ages who came from all over Europe to make new lives for themselves in the *bastides*.

There have been changes to farming as well. Sadly, the sheep have gone from the hills: they are no longer economically viable. On the other hand, more Gascon cows have been introduced in an attempt at re-establishing the breed. Profitable crops of maize now cover more land than ever. The vineyards are benefiting from greater investment and the wines are becoming known and appreciated farther afield. Even though two-thirds of all the Armagnac produced never leaves Gascony, more is now being

242

exported, to the rest of France and abroad, bringing in revenue and broadening its appeal.

Of all the ancient provinces of France, Gascony is among those that have best preserved their distinctive traits and still have a recognisable face. Life there has a deep sense of coherence and civility. People come and go about their business quietly and steadily. Nothing is pretentious or contrived. The people know the value of balancing the exploitation of the land with the need to respect it. The houses, farmsteads, fields, trees, even the colour of the soil and the Gascon cows, all blend together naturally. The peaceful, gentle valleys convey a timeless, restful quality. At sunset in summer, the western sky turns melting shades of soft amber and purple. All seems settled and at ease with itself. This is a land where you have to remind yourself – if you want to – that the outside world exists. Like strong, tannic Madiran wine, the feeling for Gascony improves with keeping.

In London one time, with my head full of thoughts of Gascony, I called in at the Comptoir Gascon to buy some Madiran. They had a couple of bottles of vintage Château Vézac, from the very year I'd gone with Old Georges to see the vineyards. The wine seller assured me this was a good year, *une très bonne année*. How could I disagree? I bought a bottle to take home.

Opening the Madiran was like letting the genie out of the bottle. It was as if the essence of Gascony – the sights and smells, the characters and places – was contained in the wine. As I drank, I remembered the visit to Château Vézac, Old Georges, Monsieur Vézac and the barrel maker. Then I thought about the Auberge, the farm, Jacques-Henri, Marie-Jeanne, Paul, Bruno, Nicolas,

243

Pattes and Anja. The smell of the soil, the colour of the earth, the shape of the hills, the golden sunshine, the warmth of the people, the noise of the *bandas* – all of them were condensed in the Madiran. Rich, full, fruity and mellow, the wine expressed my love for Gascony. I thought about the years that had passed and resolved to write down my experiences of that summer, lest I forget them for good.

# SUMMER WORK IN GASCONY

For those interested in following in my footsteps, these are some useful websites:

- www.anpe.fr (French national employment agency with 600 regional offices, useful for grape-picking and other agricultural work, indicates times of harvests)
- www.apcon.nl (grape-picking work, Netherlands based)
- www.wwoof.org (organic farming organisation)
- www.agriplanete.com (*stagiaire* posts on farms throughout France)
- www.anjoumyrtilles.fr (soft fruit picking)
- www.soldive.fr (agricultural labour)
- www.lhotellerie.fr (jobs in hotel and catering)
- www.cidj.com (youth information centres)
- www.hennessy-cognac.com (employs English-speaking guides)

And a selection of books:

- *Summer Jobs Abroad*, edited by David Woodward & Victoria Pybus, updated annually, published by Vacation Work, distributed in USA by Globe Pequot Press, Guilford, Connecticut. General information, advice and direct contact details of potential employers arranged by sector. An updated version of the list on which the *stagiaire* posts at the Auberge in Péguilhan were first advertised, compiled by Vacation Work Ltd in Oxford.

- *Live and Work in France*, by Victoria Pybus, published by Vacation Work, fifth edition 2005, distributed in USA by Globe Pequot Press, Guilford, Connecticut. Comprehensive guide to life in France; useful cultural, legal and finance information.
- *Studying and Working in France: A Student Guide*, by Russell Cousins, Ron Hallmark & Ian Pickup, Manchester University Press, second edition, 2007. An overview for EU and US students.

The ability to communicate in French is an advantage.

# HEAD OVER HEEL
## SEDUCED BY SOUTHERN ITALY
### CHRIS HARRISON

A whitewashed fishing village, a shapely signorina and an infatuated young man – head over heels on the heel of the boot. This is Chris Harrison's hilarious and captivating story of leaving his previous life for La Dolce Vita – or rather the Southern Italian version of that seductive way of life, with its luscious foods, physical beauty and sun-drenched vistas.

On a trip to Dublin, Chris falls head over heels in love with Daniela and follows her to her small home town of Andrano on the coast of Puglia. Among olive groves and cobblestone lanes, he takes us on a moving, insightful and often hilarious journey into the heart of Southern Italy. Along the way he introduces us to a cast of eccentric characters: a policeman who rearranges crimes to suit the necessary forms, a doctor who prescribes patients his homemade lemon liqueur, and – the biggest challenge of all – Daniela's *mamma*, who's determined to convert Chris to the Catholic faith, supervise his choice of underwear, and build a second storey on her stucco home where the couple might live happily ever after.

Can this relationship with Southern Italy possibly survive or will the sweet life turn sour?

*Chris Harrison is a London-based journalist and English teacher. He has written for many publications, including the* Sydney Morning Herald, The Age, The Courier Mail *and* Sports Illustrated. *A keen sportsman, he is also a qualified aerobatics pilot.* Head Over Heel *is the winner of the Grollo Ruzzene Foundation Prize. Visit www.chrisharrisonwriting.com.*

**UK only £9.99**
**Paperback Original 978 1 85788 521 7**
**320pp 216x135mm**